The PEGAN DIET COOKBOOK

Learn The *Eat Your Medicine* Approach Combining
The **Best of Paleo** and **Vegan** Diet For Absolute Lifelong Health

Renee Williams

© **Copyright 2021 - All rights reserved.**

The content contained within this book may not be reproduced, duplicated or transmitted without direct writ- ten permission from the author or the publisher. Under no circumstances will any blame or legal responsibility be held against the publisher, or author, for any damages, reparation, or monetary loss due to the information contained within this book. Either directly or indirectly.

Legal Notice:

This book is copyright protected. This book is only for personal use. You cannot amend, distribute, sell, use, quote or paraphrase any part, or the content within this book, without the consent of the author or publisher.

Disclaimer Notice:

Please note the information contained within this document is for educational and entertainment purposes only. All effort has been executed to present accurate, up to date, and reliable, complete information. No warranties of any kind are declared or implied. Readers acknowledge that the author is not engaging in the rendering of legal, financial, medical or professional advice. The content within this book has been derived from various sources. Please consult a licensed professional before attempting any techniques outlined in this book. By reading this document, the reader agrees that under no circumstances is the author responsible for any losses, direct or indirect, which are incurred as a result of the use of information contained within this document, including, but not limited to, errors, omissions, or inaccuracies.

THIS IS YOUR TABLE
of contents

BRUNCH — 13
- Cinnamon Banana Waffles — 13
- Avocado & cod fillet Toast — 13
- Cinnamon Rolls and — 14
- Cashew Spread — 14
- Vegan Poppy Seed Scones — 15
- Berries & pistachio Butter Oats — 15
- Garlic Okra Casserole — 16
- Artichoke Filled Aubergine — 16
- Açaí Bowl — 17
- Zucchini Gratin — 17
- Berries & almond Butter Oats — 18

APPETIZER — 20
- Tandoori Chickpeas — 20
- Kidney Bean Tasty Dip — 21
- Panko Air-Fried Ravioli — 22
- Cumin Sweet Potato Tots — 23
- Crispy Avocado Slices — 24
- Asian Roasted Almonds — 24
- Kale Crunchy Chips — 25
- Air-Fried Vegan Buffalo Cauliflower Wings — 26
- Almond Butter Baked Potatoes — 27

LUNCH — 29
- Garlic Lentils Casserole — 29
- Spicy Cauliflower Tacos — 30
- Tamari chicken with Mushrooms — 31
- Taste of India Bowl — 32
- Royal Chickpea Sandwich — 33
- Tasty Artichoke & White Bean Sandwich — 34
- Green Chicken Sandwich — 35
- Tacos with Tahini — 36
- Lime Quinoa & chicken Salad — 37
- Special Veggie Salad with veal — 38
- Lentils, Farro & Mustard Salad — 39
- Greek Fantasy Bowl — 40
- Chickpea Bonanza Salad Bites — 41
- Avocado & Chickpeas — 42
- Summer Cups — 42

- Pumpkin & Mushroom Risotto — 43
- Sweet Energy Potato Sushi — 44
- Classic Vegan Burritos — 45

BURGERS — 47
- Pumpkin Burgers — 47
- Balsamic Beet Burger — 48
- Black Beans Burger — 49
- Coco-Cauliflower Burgers — 50
- Simple Sweet Potato Burgers — 51
- Paprika & Almond Butter Potato Patties — 52
- Lentil & Carrot Burgers — 53
- Tumeric Beans Burger — 54
- Mushroom salmon Spicy Burger — 55
- Soy and Mustard Seitan Burgers — 56
- Spinach Flax Meal Burgers — 57
- Tempeh & Black Beans Patties — 58

WRAPS — 60
- Minty Tandory beef Wraps — 60
- Hummus and Olive Wrap — 61
- Mediterranean Vegetable Mix Wrap — 62
- Simple Lentil & Tomato Paste Wrap — 63
- Cilandrolamb Wrap with almond Sauce — 64
- Vegan Buffalo Wrap — 65
- Soy Flavoured Red Cabbage Wrap — 66
- BBQ Sauce Chikpeas Coleslaw Wrap — 67
- Curry Mango Tahini Wraps — 68
- Exotic Tofu Lettuce Wrapped — 69
- Paprika Black Bean & Quinoa Lettuce Wrap — 70

PASTA — 72
- Simple Vegetables Noodles — 72
- Spicy Vegetables Noodles with Siriracha Sauce — 73
- Classic Asian Noodles — 74
- Bok Choy Cumin Rice — 75
- Rich Pumpkin Sauce Pasta — 76
- Pasta with Pesto Sauce — 77
- Baked Pasta Bolognese & Cashew Besciamella — 78
- Chinese Vegetables Noodles — 79

SOUPS 80

Ginger & Onion Soup	80
Broccoli Avocado Cream	80
Sweet Potatoes & Legumes Soup	81
Spicy Curry Pumpkin Soup	82
Garlic Leek Soup	82
Creamy Coconut Kale Soup	83
Italian Basil & Tomato Soup	84
Garlic Beet Medley	84
Spicy Pineapple & Kale Medly	85
Aromatic Broccoli &	86
Mushroom Soup	86
Tumeric Cauliflower	87
Pakora Cream	87
Granny Herbs Veggies Soup	88

SIDES 90

Marinated Ratatouille Skewers	90
Grilled Corn with Veganaise Coating	90
Creamy Carrots Salad with Chickpeas	91
Balsamic Oven Baked Brussels Sprouts	92
Aromatic Garlic Baked Mashroom	93
Soy Sauce & Sesame Spinach	94
Curry Coated Carrots	94
Paprika Favoured Sweet Potatoes	95
Kale & Tomatoes	96
Green Beans & Mushrooms Mix	97
Yellow Squash & Bell Peppers Mix	98
Apple Flavoured Broccoli & Celery	99

PIZZA 101

Classic Italian Pizza	101
Hummus & Zucchini Summer Pizza	101
Paprika Squash Pizza with Vegetables	102
Cheesy Spinach & Red Peppers Pizza	103
Artichoke Pizza with Cashews Spread	104
Black Bean & Avocado Spicy Pizza	105
pizza base	105
BBQ turkey Pizza	106

DINNER 108

All Spices Eggplant Stew	108
BBQ Grits & Greens	109
Vegan Chili	110
Sautéed Chickpea Stew	111
Vegetables & Lentil Medley	112
Classic Asian Chana Masala	113
Chef's Favourite Ratatouille	114

SHAKES 116

Summer Strawberry Shake	116
Chocolate Coffee Power Shake	116
Greek Yogurt Exotic Shake	117
Coco Almond Fresh Smoothie	117
Vanilla Blueberries fresh Shake	118
Protein Shake for Athletes	118
Sweet Pink Smoothie	119
Fresh Green and Lean Shake	119
Kale Healthy Smoothie	120
Cinnamon Shake	120
Vegan Tofu Smoothie	121
Sunny Exotic Smoothie	121
Green Energy Shake	122
Anti-Ageing Treasure	122
Coco Turmeric Juice	123
Acai Recharge Shake	123
Skin Glow Super Shake	124
Breakfast Power Shake	124
Lemony Minty Berries	125
Healthy Veggie Juice	125

DESSERTS 127

Coco-Cinnamon Balls	127
walnut apple bake	128
Cashew-Chocolate Truffles	129
Banana ChocoCupcakes	130
Fruit Salad With Mint Scent	131
Mango Coconut Cream Pie	132
berries Vanilla Rice Pudding	133
Coconut Chia Pudding with Lime	134
After 8 Special Sorbet	134
Peach-Mango Crumble	135
Energy Bites 1 - Cranberry	136
Energy Bites 2 - Almonds & Dates	137
Pumpkin Pie Cups	138
Brownies with Raspberries	139
Coconut-Banana Pudding	140
Caramelized Bananas	141
Spiced Apple Chia Pudding	141
Sweet & Salted Fudge	142
Coco Balls	143
Choco Vanilla Cake	144
VANILLA BANANA CAKE	145
Homemade CocoBanana Ice Cream	146
Healthy Butter-Clouds Cookies	146
Spiced Apple Chia Pudding	147

FROM THE AUTHOR

Sometimes you need a new approach to things.
You've tried different roads, then experience teaches you to get the best of each world.

Sometimes life finds its balance in a hue.
Those beautiful peachy salmon shoes, That cobalt emerald lake.

Often truth stands in the middle.
The wisest choice is to take the best from both parts in order to advance faster.

This are the principles of the Pegan Diet. Thanks to this revolutionary diet, you will be able to get the best parts of two of the most popular contemporary dietary regimen: the Paleo Diet and the Vegan Diet.

SOMETIMES YOU NEED A NEW APPROACH TO THINGS.

INTRODUCTION
to Pegan Diet

WHAT IS PEGAN DIET?

We all know the benefits to our organism that a whole food diet provides: minerals, vitamins, nutrients and phytonutrients. But are whole foods the best option for any of us? In the wide range of food given at our disposal by Mother Nature modern dietary practices and studies have shown that there are differences in whole foods and also in how our own personal biology is formed. The biochemical differences between each of us, in fact, make the answer to this question impossible to be univocal. This is why today one of the best dietitian practices we have is the relatively new Pegan Diet.

The Pegan Diet is an eating philosophy created by Dr. Mark Hyman, and has been conceived to be a hybrid eating regiment between the Paleo Diet and the Vegan Diet, two of the most followed anti-inflammatory approaches to eating healthy. The starting concept is: it is possible to combine the best traits of both diets, making them work together while minimizing the negative aspects of both.
So the Pegan Diet, a mixture of the best modern anti-inflammatory diet, is born. In short, it consists in low processed whole foods that is able to reduce body inflammation and balance sugar in out blood.
But before diving into more specifics - and the best recipes you can find on "Peganism" - let's take a look at both of the two diets the Pegan comes from.

THE PALEO DIET

The Paleo diet has always been a much discussed dietary regimen, not without controversy. Studies have shown that implementing a full Paleo diet for at least ten days can lead to improve blood pressure and its glucose tolerance, reducing insuline levels.
From this diet comes the often wrong conception of the Pegan diet shouldn't contain meat. Instead Pegan, as the Paleo, suggest some meat, organic sand unprocessed, meat, fish and poultry, as essential components to our weekly meal plan.
Since this diet excludes legumes, whole grains (beside dairy, soy and any processed sugar), there has always been concerns for its followers to not get enough fibers, so that it requires to eat a lot of vegetable and fruit to make up for them. Another concern is overdoing protein, and excesses of natural sugars.

TASTY!

THE VEGAN DIET

Going Vegan is one of the most followed trend in the eating business of the last 2 decades, and substantial research demonstrates plenty of advantages associated in consuming a vegan diet. Some of the benefits are low level of inflammation, improved cardiovascular system, decreased risk of cancer, facilitated weight loss, and improved sensitivity to insuline. Obviously it excludes any kind of meat, or animal originated food, and this way of eating does not work for everyone. Many people in fact feel better after having incorporated in their diet lean and clean sources of animal protein back into their eating habits. It really depends on our biology, but it's a quite known fact that vegans have quite often a hard time to implement adequate protein, on the other hand overdoing the carbs intake, that leads to the logic extreme exclusion of any kind of sugar in the diet.

THINGS
in common

There are actually some significant points in common between the well known vegan diet and the Paleo diet. In these traits we discover an ample middle ground where the benefits of both diets can contribute to give us the best of both worlds:

- Are low in sugar, flour and refined carbohydrates
- Prefer the consumption of many vegetables and fruits;
- Are low in antibiotics, pesticides and hormones. None of the diets allow GNO foods.
- Opt organic and fresh food.
- Opt for great quality fats such as olive oil, nuts, seeds, and avocados;
- Allow no additives nor chemicals.
- Are high in protein which is great for muscle synthesis and help with appetite too.

THE PEGAN DIET: EAT YOUR MEDICINE

The "Eat your medicine" principle so dear to the Pegan diet re-establishes the old saying "You are what you eat". What we choose to introduce in our body today is extremely important and WILL (physically, biologically, practically) be what WE are constituted of in our near future.
Getting the best part from two of the best diets around makes the Pegan diet the most common sense diet, form the health paint of view, because it provides proved solid nutrition foundation. The universal fundamentals of this diets are:
- Eat whole foods that are minimally processed
- Limit your added sugar intake
- Eat lots of vegetables (but not exclusively!)
- Eat a high fiber diet

The less restrictions of this diets's principles, and its effectiveness, make this diet one of the most loved in the dietitians' contemporary scenes. While the majority of food - 75% of your intake - allowed come naturally from seasonal non-starchy vegetables (but also fruit consumption is encouraged, without going overboard), meat and eggs are a critical component of a Pegan Diet, and especially critical is the quality of the meat consumed. The diet recommend to eat lean, organic poultry, organic eggs, and grass-fed organic meat. Only by taking great care of the quality of the meat we ingest we are sure to not nullify the anti-inflammatory goals we are working hard to reach. For that and also digestion reasons we suggest to eat high quality meat two days a week, and the quantity of the meat per meal should be contained in the palm of your hand. You should get yourself used to think about meat as a side dish, not the main course.

As per dairy, just like the Paleo and Vegan diets, Pegan suggests to avoid or to consume a limited quantity dairy products. Instead of milk, yoghurt, cheese, butter and cream you can introduce in your diet coconut milk, almond yoghurt and cashew cheese.

Soy is a main nutrient of the Vegan diet but it is forbidden in Paleo; in the Pegan soy is allowed only if it comes from whole unprocessed sources like tofu, edamame or miso.
Fish is a great source of Omega-3 and as such fish rich in this nutrient should be consumed and preferred to other source of protein. We can find Omega-3 in salmon, herring, oyster, cod for example, while we should try to avoid possible source of mercury such as tuna or swordfish.

Small portions of legumes are allowed. Beside meat, side dishes can also be made of chickpeas and hummus, black and kidney beans. Whole grains are included only if they are gluten free, like brown rice, quinoa. Avoid starchy beans, and cook your lentils thoroughly to make them easily digestible.

As per sugars, Pegan Diet recommend to strongly limit its consumption, both processed or unprocessed if possible. better after having incorporated in their diet lean and clean sources of animal protein back into their eating habits. It really depends on our biology, but it's a quite known fact that vegans have quite often a hard time to implement adequate protein, on the other hand overdoing the carbs intake, that leads to the logic extreme exclusion of any kind of sugar in the diet.

WHAT CAN YOU EAT?

The food you can eat:
- Fruit: apples, berries, oranges, bananas, pears etc.
- Vegetables: cauliflower, asparagus, leafy greens, broccoli, celery etc.
- Grains (in small amounts): quinoa, oats, brown rice, buckwheat, millet, sorghum, tapioca.
- Legumes (in small amounts): chickpeas, black beans, pinto beans, kidney beans, lentils
- Nuts/seeds: almonds, walnuts, cashews, pistachios, macadamia nuts, chia seeds, flaxseed, hemp seed
- Wild-caught fish: salmon, sardines, anchovies, mackerel, tuna, etc.
- Grass-fed meat: beef, venison, lamb, etc.
- Free-range poultry: chicken, turkey, duck, goose, etc.
- Cage-free eggs
- Healthy fats: unrefined coconut oil, avocado oil, olive oil
- Herbs/spices: cumin, cinnamon, cilantro, oregano, basil, turmeric, etc.

Food to avoid:
- Conventional farmed meat, poultry, seafood and eggs
- Dairy products: milk, yogurt, cheese, butter, ghee, etc.
- Grains: gluten-containing grains, such as wheat and barley
- Legumes: peanuts
- Refined oils: sunflower oil, corn oil, soybean oil, canola oil
- Sugar and sugar-sweetened products
- Processed foods: chips, crackers, cookies, convenience meals, pretzels, granola bars, refined grains, fast food

WHY GO GLUTEN-FREE?

Since gluten may cause inflammation and digestive complications, the Pegan diet only allows gluten-free grains such as quinoa, brown rice, wild rice, oats and few more. The regulated consumption of these glycemic grains is a great source of protein and vitamins.

BENEFITS OF THE DIET

By combining two of the healthier diets around, the Pegan Diet can be expected to have positive effect and extensive health benefits when used properly. For once, eating lots of vegetables will make up for any lack of fibers and vitamins that the average American diet usually have. In addition, those who suffer of diabetic condition can take benefits from the low sugar the Pegan Diet propose in order to control the sugar level in blood.

One of the often most underestimated pros of a Pegan Diet is its low environmental impact. With the promotion of consuming - and purchasing - only sustainable and organic meat, and reducing its consumption in general, this diet gives a great hand to our planet.

A regular healthy diet can help you stay healthy and fit, and if you measure the calories and burn more calories than you eat this can lead to losing weight. Of course this will have be accompanied to a well balanced routine of physical exercise, to be decided with a professional, depending on our age and physical possibilities. Moreover it can help treat and prevent many forms of chronic disease. As you'll see soon in the recipes, the Pegan Diet is one of the most sustainable diets around, for the range of food allowed and the possibility of great tasting meals it offers, and that is the reason why today it is also one of the most successful and used diet.

BRUNCH RECIPES

CINNAMON BANANA WAFFLES

 5 MINUTES    5 MINUTES   6 SERVINGS

INGREDIENTS

- 1 tablespoon baking powder
- 2 tablespoon sugar
- 1 teaspoon ground cinnamon
- 2 1/2 tablespoon cashew butter
- 200g all-purpose flour
- 1/4 teaspoon baking soda
- 1/4 teaspoon ground nutmeg
- 1 peeled medium banana
- 1 cup cashew milk, unsweetened

HOW TO MAKE IT

1. Put all the ingredients in a blender: on the list, cashew milk and baking powder first. Puree for one minute until the mixture is smooth.

2. Using a spoon, transfer the mixture to a waffle iron and bake over medium-high heat. The appliance may not tell you when they are ready. Remove the waffle from the iron when you can no longer see any steam.

Nutrition
291 calories | 13g fat | 3g protein

AVOCADO & COD FILLET TOAST

 5 MINUTES    0 MINUTES    4 SERVINGS

INGREDIENTS

- 1 tbsp. lemon juice
- 4 lettuce leaves
- 2 tbsp. green olive paste
- 1 avocado, halved, peeled and finely chopped
- 1 tbsp. green onions, finely chopped
- 50 gr. fresh Cod fillet (optional)
- 4 slices of gluten free bread

HOW TO MAKE IT

1. Mash the avocados with a fork or potato masher until they are almost smooth. Include the onions, green olive paste and lemon juice. Add salt and pepper to taste. Stir to combine.

2. Grab a griddle pan, grease lightly with olive oil if needed and place your cod fillet once the pan is hot. Let it cook for 4 minutes on each side. Remove from the pan and cut into smaller piecer or shred the fillet.

3. Take 4 slices of gluten free bread and toast until golden brown. Drop 1/4 of the avocado mixture onto each slice of bread, top with a lettuce leaf and shred cod. Serve.

Nutrition
Calories: 200 | Carbs: 35g | Protein: 4g | Fat: 5g

CINNAMON ROLLS AND CASHEW SPREAD

BRUNCH

14

 25 MINUTES    25 MINUTES    12 SERVINGS

INGREDIENTS

- 2/3 cup almond milk
- 1 teaspoon vanilla extract
- 1/2 teaspoon salt
- 3 tablespoons caster sugar
- 1 teaspoon vanilla extract
- 1/2 cup pumpkin puree
- 3/4 cup unsweetened almond milk
- 3 cups almond flour
- 1/2 cup icing sugar
- 3 tablespoons softened vegan butter
- 3 tablespoons brown sugar
- 1/2 teaspoon cinnamon
- 2 1/4 teaspoons dried active yeast
- 1/2 cup cashews
- 3 tablespoons vegan butter

HOW TO MAKE IT

1. Let the cashews soak in boiling water for 1 hour. Butter a baking tray and put it aside. Locate a small bowl, and add the butter and melt it in the microwave.

2. Pour in the sugar, give it a good stir and set aside to cool.

3. In a large bowl, add the flour, salt and yeast. Mix well to combine them. Place the cooled butter in a jug, add the pumpkin puree, vanilla and almond milk. Mix everything together well. Then pour the wet ingredients into the dry ingredients and stir well.

4. Tip dough onto a flat surface and knead for 5 minutes, adding extra flour as needed so it doesn't stick. Put back into the bowl, covered with cling film and place in the fridge overnight.

5. Remove the dough from the fridge and press it down with your fingers. Using a rolling pin, turn the dough out into an 18-inch rectangle and brush with butter.

6. In a small bowl, take the sugar and cinnamon and add them. Combine well and then sprinkle with the butter. Then roll the dough into a large sausage and slice it into sections.

7. Put the dough on the greased baking sheet and let it rise in a dark place for an hour.

8. Preheat the oven to 350°F. Let the cashews drain and put them in your blender. Puree them until they are smooth.

9. Next, add the sugar and vanilla and blend again. Allow the almond milk to be added until the desired consistency is reached.

10. Place the cake in the oven and bake for 20 minutes until golden brown. Drizzle the glaze over the top, serve and enjoy.

Nutrition Calories 243 | Fat 9 | Carbs 34 | Protein 4

BRUNCH

VEGAN POPPY SEED SCONES

 5 MINUTES    10 MINUTES    12 SERVINGS

INGREDIENTS

- 1/2 teaspoon salt
- 1 cup Earth Balance or vegan butter
- 1/2 cup soy milk
- Juice from 1 lemon
- Zest from 1 lemon
- 1 cup white sugar
- 2 tablespoon poppy seeds
- 4 teaspoon baking powder
- 2 cups oat flour
- 1/3 cup water

HOW TO MAKE IT

1. First, preheat the oven to 400 degrees. Mix the sugar, flour, powder and salt in a large mixing bowl next. Then add the vegan butter to the mixture and grind it until you get a sand-like mixture.

2. Now add the lemon juice, lemon zest and poppy seeds. Then pour in the water and the soy milk and mix well. 3.

3. Divide the dough into about 1/4 cup portions on a baking tray. Allow the scones to bake for fifteen minutes. Let them cool before serving. Enjoy.

Nutrition   Calories 205 | Fat 3 | Carbs 12 | Protein 6

BERRIES & PISTACHIO BUTTER OATS

 10 MINUTES    25 MINUTES   2 SERVINGS

INGREDIENTS

- 1 tablespoon pistachio butter
- 1 teaspoon vegan syrup
- 80g frozen raspberries
- 50g rolled porridge oats

HOW TO MAKE IT

1. 1. Mix the frozen raspberries with your oatmeal.
2. 2. Add 150 ml of water and a pinch of salt.
3. 3. Put a lid on and refrigerate overnight.
4. 4. Next, combine the maple syrup and top with the oatmeal and pistachio butter.

Nutrition

Calories: 205 | Fat: 3g | Carbs: 12g | Protein: 2g

GARLIC OKRA CASSEROLE

 25 MINUTES    45 MINUTES    4 SERVINGS

INGREDIENTS

- 1 cup fresh parsley leaves, finely cut
- 3 garlic cloves, chopped
- 1 lb. okra, trimmed
- 3 tomatoes, cut into wedges

NUTRITION

302 calories | 13g fat | 6g protein

HOW TO MAKE IT

1. Combine okra, sliced tomatoes, olive oil and garlic in a deep ovenproof casserole dish.
2. Add salt and black pepper to taste and stir through to combine.
3. Cook okra in prepared oven at 350 F for 45 minutes.
4. Decorate with parsley and serve.

ARTICHOKE FILLED AUBERGINE

 10 MINUTES    25 MINUTES    2 SERVINGS

INGREDIENTS

- 1/4 cup artichoke hearts, chopped
- 2 tablespoon red bell pepper, diced 1 cup spinach
- Large Aubergine
- 1/4 medium yellow onion, diced
- 1 egg (optional)

NUTRITION

Calories: 307 | Fat: 21g | Carbs: 2.5g | Protein: 1.5g

HOW TO MAKE IT

1. Slice the aubergine lengthways and scoop out the flesh, leaving a skin about half a centimetre thick. Shred it and put it aside.
2. Set a frying pan over medium heat and spray with cooking spray. Boil the onions for about three to five minutes until they are soft.
3. Then include the peppers, spinach, artichokes and aubergine flesh. Roast for another five minutes and then take off the heat. Mix in the egg.
4. Ladle this mixture equally into the aubergine shells and put each into the oven. Let it cook at 250° C until the aubergine shells are soft. Serve warm.

BRUNCH

ZUCCHINI GRATIN

 5 MINUTES    10 MINUTES    2 SERVINGS

INGREDIENTS

- 1 teaspoon vegan butter, melted
- 2 zucchini
- 1 tablespoon dried parsley
- 5 oz. vegan cheese, shredded
- 1 tablespoon coconut flour

NUTRITION

Calories: 209 | Fat: 12g | Carbs: 17g | Protein: 5g

HOW TO MAKE IT

1. Combine cheese and coconut flour in a bowl and season with some parsley to flavour.
2. Halve the courgettes lengthways and cut the halves into four slices.
3. Heat the deep fryer to 400 degrees.
4. Drizzle the melted butter over the courgette and then dunk the courgette in the cheese and flour mixture so that they are covered all around.
5. Fry the courgettes in the deep fryer for thirteen minutes.

AÇAÍ BOWL

 10 MINUTES    35 MINUTES   2 SERVINGS

INGREDIENTS

- 1/2 a very ripe banana chopped
- Handful ice cubes
- 2 teaspoon açai powder
- Handful frozen berries
- 1/2 passion fruit
- 1 teaspoon coconut flakes
- 5 pineapple chunks
- 1 tablespoon toasted oats, to top

HOW TO MAKE IT

1. Put the açai powder, frozen berries, banana and ice cubes in a blender. Add 100 ml of water.
2. Mix until everything is smooth.
3. Dump the mixture in a bowl and garnish with toppings of your choice.

NUTRITION

Nutrition: Calories: 405 | Fat: 11g | Carbs: 2g | Protein: 2g

BRUNCH

BERRIES & ALMOND BUTTER OATS

10 MINUTES | 25 MINUTES | 2 SERVINGS

INGREDIENTS

- 1 tablespoon almond butter
- 1 teaspoon vegan syrup
- 80g frozen raspberries
- 50g rolled porridge oats

HOW TO MAKE IT

1. 1. Mix the frozen raspberries with your oatmeal.
2. 2. Add 150 ml of water and a pinch of salt.
3. 3. Put a lid on and refrigerate overnight.
4. 4. Next, combine the maple syrup and top with the oatmeal and almond butter.

Nutrition Calories: 205 | Fat: 3g | Carbs: 12g | Protein: 2g

APPETIZERS

19

TANDOORI CHICKPEAS

 5 MINUTES    20 MINUTES    4 SERVINGS

INGREDIENTS

- 1 tablespoon olive oil
- 2 teaspoons tandoori spice blend
- 19 ounces cooked chickpeas
- 3/4 teaspoon salt
- 300g/10½oz cherry tomatoes
- 1 tbsp tomato purée
- ½ tsp ground turmeric
- 2 tsp cumin seeds
- 2 tsp coriander seeds

HOW TO MAKE IT

1. Preheat the oven to 170C/150C
2. Meanwhile, roughly crush the cumin and coriander seeds, place them in a big bowl, add the chickpeas, the rest of the ingredients and stir until mixed.
3. Pour the mixture in a ovenproof saute pan and cover with a lid. Cook in the oven for 1¼ hours.
4. Stir once halfway through the cooking time. When ready remove carefully from the oven and serve.

NUTRITION   Calories: 140 | Fat: 5 g | Carbs: 17 g | Protein: 6 g | Fiber: 4 g

KIDNEY BEAN TASTY DIP

 10 MINUTES   10 MINUTES 4 SERVINGS

INGREDIENTS

- 1 onion, chopped
- 2 tablespoons olive oil
- 1 bell pepper, chopped
- 2 cups red kidney beans, boiled and drained
- 2 cloves garlic, minced
- 1/4 cup olive oil
- 2 tablespoons fresh parsley, chopped
- 1 teaspoon stone-ground mustard
- Sea salt and ground black pepper, to taste
- 2 tablespoons fresh basil, chopped

HOW TO MAKE IT

1. In a skillet, heat the oil over medium-high flame.
2. Pour in the onion, the garlic and the pepper for about 3 minutes (make sure they are tender).
3. Place the sautéed mixture to your blender and combine the rest of the ingredients.
4. Blend all the ingredients in your blender or food processor until smooth and creamy.
5. Serve with sweet potatoes chips.

NUTRITION Calories: 135; Fat: 12.1g; Carbs: 4.4g; Protein: 1.6g

PANKO AIR-FRIED RAVIOLI

 5 MINUTES    24 MINUTES    4 SERVINGS

INGREDIENTS

- 2 teaspoons nutritional yeast
- Olive oil spray
- 1 teaspoon dried oregano
- 1/4 cup chickpeas liquid
- 1/4 teaspoon ground black pepper
- 1/2 cup marinara
- 1/4 teaspoon salt
- 1/2 cup panko bread crumbs
- 8 ounces frozen vegan ravioli, thawed
- 1 teaspoon dried basil
- 1 teaspoon garlic powder

HOW TO MAKE IT

1. Turn on the hot air fryer, insert the frying basket, cover with the lid, adjust the frying temperature to 390 degrees F and preheat for 5 minutes.

2. In the meantime, place breadcrumbs in a shallow bowl, include nutritional yeast and all the herbs and spices and mix until blended.

3.

4. Grab a bowl, pour in the chickpea liquid, submerge the ravioli in it and coat them in the breadcrumb mixture until they are evenly coated.

5. Crack open the preheated air fryer, put the ravioli inside, drizzle with olive oil, shut the lid and cook for 12 minutes until golden brown and done, turning and spraying with oil halfway through.

6. At the end of cooking, the deep fryer will beep, then open the lid, put the ravioli on a plate and cover with foil to keep warm.

7. Prepare the remaining ravioli in the same way and then serve immediately.

NUTRITION   Calories: 150 | Cal Fat: 2 g | Carbs: 27 g | Protein: 5 g | Fiber: 2 g

CUMIN SWEET POTATO TOTS

5 MINUTES | 28 MINUTES | 25 SERVINGS

INGREDIENTS

- Olive oil spray
- 1/2 teaspoon salt
- 2 cups sweet potato in cubes
- 1/2 teaspoon ground coriander
- 1/2 teaspoon ground cumin
- 1 cup panko bread crumbs

HOW TO MAKE IT

1. Make holes in the sweet potatoes with a fork and bake in the oven at 400-degree F (204 C) until soft.

2. When the potatoes are done, take a large bowl and mash them. Add all the ingredients in, stir until well mixed, then shape the mixture into twenty-five tots, about 1 tablespoon each. Roll them in panko bread crumbs.

3. Preheat oven to 375 degrees F (190 C). Spray a baking sheet with nonstick spray. Adjust the tots on top.

4. Bake for 20 minutes, then gently flip. Bake for 20 minutes more then serve immediately.

NUTRITION Calories: 26 Cal | Fat: 0.2 g | Carbs: 6 g | Protein: 0 g | Fiber: 2 g

ASIAN ROASTED ALMONDS

 5 MINUTES    6 MINUTES    8 SERVINGS

INGREDIENTS

- 1 tablespoon soy sauce
- 1 teaspoon paprika
- 2 cups almonds
- 1/4 teaspoon ground black pepper
- 1 tablespoon garlic powder

NUTRITION

Calories: 7.7 Cal Fat: 0.7 g Carbs: 0.3 g Protein: 0.3 g Fiber: 0.1 g

HOW TO MAKE IT

1. Preheat oven to 325 degrees.
2. Meanwhile, get a large bowl, add the almonds, then the rest of the ingredients and toss until mixed.
3. Line a large, baking tray with parchment paper and adjust the almonds on a single layer.
4. Roast whole almonds in preheated oven for 9-12 minutes.

CRISPY AVOCADO SLICES

 5 MINUTES    10 MINUTES    4 SERVINGS

INGREDIENTS

- 1/4 cup chickpeas liquid
- Olive oil spray
- 1/2 cup panko breadcrumbs
- 1 medium avocado, peeled, pitted, sliced
- 1/2 teaspoon salt

NUTRITION

Calories: 132 Cal Fat: 11.1 g Carbs: 6.6 g Protein: 4 g Fiber: 4 g

HOW TO MAKE IT

1. Pre-heat oven to 400 Degrees F. Pour 1 tablespoon oil on a no stick tray. Meanwhile, get a shallow bowl, put the breadcrumbs in it, flavour with salt and stir until combined.
2. Grab another shallow bowl, add the chickpea liquid, submerge the avocado slices in it and then dredge them in the breadcrumb coating until they are coated.
3. Adjust the slices on the tray and bake for 15 minutes or until the avocados are golden and crispy.
4. Serve with a dip of your likings.

KALE CRUNCHY CHIPS

 5 MINUTES   5 MINUTES   2 SERVINGS

INGREDIENTS

- 2 tablespoons olive oil
- 1 tablespoon nutritional yeast
- 2 teaspoons ranch seasoning, vegan
- 4 cups kale leaves, stems removed
- 1/4 teaspoon salt

HOW TO MAKE IT

1. Preheat an oven to 350 degrees F (175 degrees C). Line a sheet of parchment paper on a baking tray.
2. In the meantime, take a medium sized bowl, place the kale leaves and the rest of the ingredients and stir until coated.
3. Bake until the edges brown but are not burnt, 10 to 15 minutes.
4. Serve immediately.

NUTRITION

Calories: 98 Cal Fat: 4 g Carbs: 15.7 g Protein: 0 g Fiber: 2.7 g

APPETIZER
AIR-FRIED VEGAN BUFFALO CAULIFLOWER WINGS

10 MINUTES   40 MINUTES   4 SERVINGS

INGREDIENTS

- 1/4 teaspoon dried chipotle chili
- 1 large head cauliflower, cut into florets
- 1 cup almond flour
- 2 tablespoons almond butter
- 1 cup of soy milk
- 1/2 cup Frank red hot sauce

Olive oil spray For the Batter:

- 1 teaspoon minced garlic
- 1/4 teaspoon red chili powder
- 1/4 teaspoon paprika
- 1 teaspoon granules of chicken bouillon, vegan
- 1/4 teaspoon cayenne pepper

HOW TO MAKE IT

1. Turn on the hot air fryer, insert the frying basket, close it with the lid, set the frying temperature to 390 degrees F and preheat for 5 minutes.

2. In meantime, prepare the batter. To do this, get a large bowl, add all the ingredients and whisk the batter until it is smooth.

3. Then put in the cauliflower florets and toss until they are well coated.

4. Then open the preheated deep fryer, add the cauliflower florets in a single layer, shut the lid and cook for 20 minutes until golden brown and cooked through, flipping and spraying with oil halfway through.

5. In the meantime, make the sauce. To do this, get a small saucepan, set it over medium-high heat, throw in the butter, stir in the garlic and hot sauce, and bring the mixture to the boil, then let it simmer over medium heat until thickened and finally cover the saucepan.

6. When the cauliflower is done, the fryer will beep, and then open the lid, put the cauliflower florets in a large bowl and keep them covered with foil to stay warm.

7. Boil the remaining cauliflower florets in the same way, transfer them to the bowl, pour the prepared sauce over and toss until well coated.

8. Serve

NUTRITION
Calories: 129 Cal Fat: 1 g Carbs: 24 g Protein: 7 g Fiber: 4 g

ALMOND BUTTER BAKED POTATOES

5 MINUTES   60 MINUTES   4 SERVINGS

INGREDIENTS

- 2 teaspoons ground black pepper
- 2 tablespoons olive oil
- 2 teaspoons salt
- 1 teaspoon garlic powder
- 4 tablespoons almond butter, divided
- 4 large baking potatoes
- 4 tablespoons chopped parsley

HOW TO MAKE IT

1. Preheat oven to 200 C degrees.
2. In the meantime, coat the potatoes with oil, season with garlic powder, salt and black pepper and sprinkle with parsley.
3. Lay the potatoes on a baking tray lightly greased and cook for about 60 minutes.
4. Cut the potatoes by halving them lengthwise, put 1 tablespoon of butter on each potato and serve.

NUTRITION Calories: 161 Cal Fat: 0.2 g Carbs: 37 g Protein: 4.3 g Fiber: 3.8 g

28

LUNCH

LUNCH

GARLIC LENTILS CASSEROLE

10 MINUTES　　35 MINUTES　　4 SERVINGS

INGREDIENTS

- 700g potatoes, peeled and cut into chunks
- 2 parsnip, thickly sliced
- 100g red lentils
- 2 garlic cloves, crushed
- 2 tbsp vegetable oil
- 2 tbsp curry paste or powder
- 1 liter/13/4 pints vegetable stock
- 1 onion, chopped
- 4 carrot, thickly sliced

HOW TO MAKE IT

1. Heat the oil in a large frying pan and fry the onion and garlic over a medium heat for 3 minutes.

2. Keep stirring in between so that they cook well. Allow the potatoes, carrots and parsnips to cook, then turn up the heat and cook for 6 to 7 minutes. Stir well.

3. Mix in the curry paste or powder, add the stock and bring to the boil. Lower the heat, add the lentils. Close the lid and let simmer for 18 minutes.

4. When cooked, add coriander and heat through for a minute. Then serve with yoghurt and the remaining coriander.

NUTRITION　378 Calories | 14g Protein | 10g Fiber

LUNCH

SPICY CAULIFLOWER TACOS

 10 MINUTES   30 MINUTES    8 SERVINGS

INGREDIENTS

- For the roasted cauliflower
- 1 head Cauliflower
- 1 tbsp Olive oil
- 2 tbsp corn Flour
- 2 tbsp Nutritional yeast
- 1 tsp Chili powder
- 2 tsp Smoked paprika
- For the tacos
- 2 cups Shredded lettuce
- Grated carrots
- 5 cups Mango salsa
- 5 cups Guacamole
- 2 cups cherry tomatoes
- 3 Lime wedges
- 8 Corn tortillas

HOW TO MAKE IT

1. Switch on the oven and let warm up to 350 degrees. Prepare a baking sheet and set aside.

2. Swirl the cauliflower with the oil and in another bowl combine all the spices before you add them to the cauliflower.

3. Distribute this on the baking tray and place it in the oven. After 20 minutes you can remove it from the oven, it will be ready.

4. When the cauliflower is cooked, you can use this and the rest of the ingredients to put the tacos together.

NUTRITION   Calories: 198 | Carbs: 32g | Fat: 6g | Protein: 7g

LUNCH

TAMARI CHICKEN WITH MUSHROOMS

 5-8 MINUTES  5 MINUTES  4 SERVINGS

INGREDIENTS

- 6 large mushrooms, sliced
- Cooking oil as needed
- 1/4 cup vegetable stock
- 1/2 cup red bell pepper
- Salt and white pepper to the taste
- 1 yellow onion, thinly sliced
- 3 teaspoons tamari
- 8 ounces Chicken, cubes (vegan: 8 ounces tofu)
- 1/2 cup green beans

HOW TO MAKE IT

1. Pick up your Instant Pot and Switch it on after plugging it into a power socket.

2. Pre heat a no stick pan, pour the oil, mushrooms and onions in the pan and cook for 2-3 minutes until the ingredients are soft.

3. Put in the tamari and chicken and cook for a further 5 minutes. Whisk in the stock and stir gently.

4. Shut the lid and lock it in place. Ensure that you have sealed the valve to prevent leakage.

5. Push the "Manual" mode and adjust the timer for 3 minutes. It will take a few minutes for the pot to build up internal pressure and begin to boil.

6. Once the timer reads zero, press "Cancel" and quickly relieve the pressure.

7. Put in the green beans and the peppers. Press "Manual" mode and put the timer on 1 minute. Once the timer reads zero, push "Cancel" and quickly release the pressure.

8. Remove the lid carefully; add the pepper and salt. Serve warm!

NUTRITION Calories 112 | Fat 6g | Carbohydrates 9g | Fiber 1.5g | Protein 7g

LUNCH

TASTE OF INDIA BOWL

5 MINUTES | 25 MINUTES | 4 SERVINGS

INGREDIENTS

- 1 cup Water
- 2 cups Vegetable broth
- 0.5 cup Diced onion
- 1 cup Chopped carrots
- 1 tsp Salt
- Diced Roma tomatoes
- 2 tsp Garam masala seasoning
- 1 cup Vegan milk
- 1.5 cup Dried red lentils
- 15 oz. Drained chickpeas
- 5 tsp Curry powder

HOW TO MAKE IT

1. Take a pot and start boiling some water and carrots. You can drain them after 5 minutes and set them aside.

2. While the carrots are cooking, start heating some oil in a pan and fry the onion. It will take about 10 minutes.

3. Now in the same pot you used to boil the carrots, place the chickpeas, carrots, milk, water, vegetable stock, lentils and onion along with the spices.

4. Heat to boiling before you reduce the heat and let the whole thing simmer for a little while.

5. After cooking for twenty minutes, you may remove the pot from the cooker. It's ready to be served and enjoyed.

NUTRITION Calories: 189 | Carbs: 22g | Fat: 11g | Protein: 16g

LUNCH

ROYAL CHICKPEA SANDWICH

 15 MINUTES  10 MINUTES  2 SERVINGS

INGREDIENTS

For The Sandwich:

- 1/2 teaspoon Dijon mustard
- 4 pieces of rustic bread
- 1/4 cup chopped red onion
- 1/2 teaspoon salt
- 1 tablespoon maple syrup
- 1 3/4 cup cooked chickpeas
- 1/4 teaspoon ground black pepper
- 3 tablespoons vegan mayonnaise
- 2 tablespoons fresh dill
- 1/4 cup roasted sunflower seeds, unsalted

For The Garlic Herb Sauce:

- 1/4 cup almond milk, unsweetened
- 1 teaspoon minced garlic
- 1/2 teaspoon of sea salt
- 1/4 dried dill
- 1/4 cup hummus
- 1 teaspoon dried dill
- 1/2 of lemon, juiced

For Topping:

- 1 medium tomato, sliced
- 1/2 cup chopped lettuce
- 1 avocado, pitted, sliced
- 1 medium white onion, peeled, sliced

HOW TO MAKE IT

1. Start this recipe by making the garlic and herb sauce. Take a medium bowl, put all the ingredients in and whisk until combined and set aside.

2. Get a medium bowl, add the chickpeas and mash them with a fork until they break down.

3. Then put in the onion, dill, sunflower seeds, salt, black pepper, mustard, maple syrup and mayonnaise and mix until everything is well combined.

4. Taking a medium frying pan, set it on medium heat, add the bread slices and fry them for 3 minutes per side until toasted.

5. Coat one side of two bread slices with the chickpea mixture, cover with the prepared garlic and herb sauce, avocado, onion, tomato and lettuce and cover with the other two slices.

6. Serve immediately.

Nutrition 532 Cal | 30 g Fat | 4 g Saturated Fat | 52 g Carbohydrates | 14 g Fiber | 8 g Sugars | 17 g Protein;

TASTY ARTICHOKE & WHITE BEAN SANDWICH

LUNCH

15 MINUTES | 10 MINUTES | 4 SERVINGS

INGREDIENTS

- 1/4 teaspoon ground black pepper
- 1 lemon, grated
- 1/2 cup cashew nuts
- 6 artichoke hearts, chopped
- 8 pieces of rustic bread
- 1 clove of garlic, peeled
- 1/4 teaspoon salt
- 1 teaspoon dried rosemary
- 1/4 cup sunflower seeds, hulled
- 6 tablespoons almond milk, unsweetened
- 1 1/4 cooked white beans

HOW TO MAKE IT

1.
2. Let the cashew nuts soak in warm water for 10 minutes, drain them and put them in a food processor.
3. Then add the garlic, salt, black pepper, rosemary, lemon zest and milk and pulse for 2 minutes until the mixture is smooth.
4. Get a medium bowl, place the beans, mash them with a fork, then add the sunflower seeds and artichokes and mix until everything is blended. Add the cashew nut dressing, mix until coated. Taste to adjust seasonings.
5. Grab a medium frying pan, put it on medium heat, place the bread slices in and fry them until toasted, 3 minutes per side.
6. Divide the white bean mixture between one side of your four slices of bread and cover with the other four slices.
7. Serve immediately.

NUTRITION 220 Cal, 8 g Fat, 1 g Saturated Fat, 28 g Carbohydrates, 8 g Fiber, 2 g Sugars, 12 g Protein

LUNCH

GREEN CHICKEN SANDWICH

 10 MINUTES    15 MINUTES   4 SERVINGS

INGREDIENTS

- 8 slices of oat sandwich bread
- 1/2 cup green pesto
- 1 1/2 teaspoon dried oregano
- 17 oz chicken (vegan: 1 steak of seitan)
- 8 slices of tomato
- 2 tablespoons olive oil
- 8 leaves of lettuce

HOW TO MAKE IT

1. Turn on the oven, set it to 375 degrees F and let it preheat.
2. Slice the chicken into slices, put them on a baking tray, sprinkle with oil and sprinkle with oregano and bake for 20 minutes.
3. Let's combine the sandwich. Spread one side of each bread slice with pesto, cover four slices with lettuce, tomato slices and chicken and top with the other four slices.
4. Serve immediately.

NUTRITION   277 Cal, 9.1 g Fat, 1.5 g Saturated Fat, 33.1 g Carbohydrates, 3.6 g Fiber, 12.7 g Sugars, 16.1 g Protein;

LUNCH

TACOS WITH TAHINI

 10 MINUTES  0 MINUTES  4 SERVINGS

INGREDIENTS

For the Filling:

- 1/2 cup alfalfa sprouts
- 1/2 cup sprouted hummus dip
- 1 tablespoon hemp seeds
- 1 head romaine lettuce, destemmed
- 3/4 cup sliced red cabbage
- 1 cup halved cherry tomatoes
- 1 medium avocado, peeled, pitted, cubed
- 1 cup shredded carrots

For the Sauce:

- 2 tablespoons lemon juice
- 3 tablespoons water
- 1/8 teaspoon sea salt
- 1 tablespoon maple syrup
- 1/3 cup tahini

HOW TO MAKE IT

1. Let's make the sauce first. Take a medium-sized bowl, add all the sauce ingredients. Stir until they are well mixed and the texture results smooth.

2. Now assemble the boats: Organise lettuce leaves into twelve portions, place the hummus and the rest of the ingredients for the stuffing on top of each leaf.

3. Serve with the sauce we made at the beginning.

NUTRITION 314 Cal, 23.6 g Fat, 4 g Saturated Fat, 23.2 g Carbohydrates, 9.3 g Fiber, 6.2 g Sugars, 8 g Protein;

LUNCH

LIME QUINOA & CHICKEN SALAD

35 MINUTES   20 MINUTES   4 SERVINGS

INGREDIENTS

For the Salad:

- 1 1/2 cup chicken, shredded (vegan: cooked black beans)
- 2 medium tomatoes, chopped
- 1 cup quinoa
- 4 tablespoons chopped cilantro
- 2 cups of water
- 1/2 cup minced red onion
- 1 cup of corn

For The Dressing:

- 2 tablespoons olive oil
- 1/4 teaspoon of sea salt
- 4 tablespoons lime juice
- 2 tablespoons lime zest

HOW TO MAKE IT

1. Get a medium saucepan, set it on medium heat, fill it with water, pour in the quinoa and bring it to the boil.

2. Switch the heat to low and cook the quinoa for 15 minutes until all the water is soaked up and the quinoa is done.

3. While the quinoa is boiling, make the dressing. Take a small bowl, add all the ingredients and mix until combined and put aside until ready to use.

4. Once the quinoa is cooked, crush it with a fork, then put it in a medium bowl and let it cool in the fridge for 30 minutes.

5. Grab a griddle pan and cook the chicken breast for about 5 minutes on each side (depends on how thick the slices are. Shred the chicken once you removed it from the pan.

6. Place the remaining ingredients for the salad with the quinoa, sprinkle with the dressing and toss until well combined. (Combine the black beans instead of the chicken you you choose the vegan alternative)

7. Serve immediately.

NUTRITION 229 Cal, 10 g Fat, 2 g Saturated Fat 27 g Carbohydrates 3 g Fiber, 2 g Sugars, 6 g Protein;

SPECIAL VEGGIE SALAD WITH VEAL

 10 MINUTES   25 MINUTES   4 SERVINGS

INGREDIENTS

For the salad:

- 2 cups chopped sweet potato, peeled
- 1 cup olive oil
- 2 cups Brussel sprout, halved
- 4 teaspoons salt
- 4 teaspoons ground black pepper
- 2 cups broccoli floret
- 15 oz Veal, diced (vegan: 2 cups chopped tofu, drained)
- 4 tablespoons red chili powder
- 2 cups cooked chickpeas
- 4 cups spinach

For the dressing:

- 1/2 cup hummus
- 2 teaspoons salt
- 4 tablespoons olive oil
- 4 tablespoons lemon juice
- 2 teaspoons water
- 2 teaspoons ground black pepper 4 teaspoons dried thyme

HOW TO MAKE IT

1. Turn on the oven, then set it to 400 degrees F and let it preheat.
2. Take a large baking tray, grease it with oil and spread broccoli florets in one-fifth portion, saving some florets for later use.
3. Put the sprouts, sweet potatoes, veal/tofu and chickpeas in a single heap on the baking tray, sprinkle with oil, spice with salt, black pepper and red chilli powder and then bake for 25 minutes until the chicken/tofu is nicely golden brown and the vegetables are soft, giving them a stir halfway through.
4. Whilst the vegetables, grains and veal are roasting, prepare the dressing. Take a medium-sized jar, add all the ingredients, mix until everything is well blended and then divide the dressing between four large canning jars.
5. Once the vegetables, grains and veal are nicely done, divide them evenly between the four canning jars along with the reserved cauliflower florets and seal with a lid.
6. Once you are ready, give the jars a good shake until the salad is coated with the dressing and then serve.

NUTRITION 477 Cal, 24 g Fat, 5 g Saturated Fat, 52 g Carbohydrates, 16 g Fiber, 11 g Sugars, 21 g Protein;

LUNCH

LENTILS, FARRO & MUSTARD SALAD

10 MINUTES   0 MINUTES   4 SERVINGS

INGREDIENTS

For the Salad:

- 1 1/2 cups lentils, cooked
- 3 1/2 cups farro, cooked
- 1/3 cup chopped parsley
- 1 cup fresh arugula
- 1 cup grape tomato, halved
- 1/2 cup diced yellow bell pepper 1 cup diced cucumber,
- 1/2 cup diced red bell pepper

For the Dressing:

- 1/4 teaspoon ground black pepper 1 teaspoon Italian seasoning
- 1/3 cup olive oil
- 2 tablespoons lemon juice
- 1/2 teaspoon salt
- 2 tablespoons red wine vinegar
- 1 teaspoon Dijon mustard
- 1/2 teaspoon minced garlic

HOW TO MAKE IT

1. Get a large bowl, add all the ingredients for the salad except the rocket and swirl until everything is well combined.
2. Make the dressing. Take a medium bowl, put all the dressing ingredients in it and mix the dressing until it is well combined.
3. Drizzle the dressing over the salad, swirl until well covered, then distribute the salad among four bowls.
4. Serve immediately.

NUTRITION   379 Cal, 10 g Fat, 2 g Saturated Fat, 63.5 g Carbohydrates, 11 g Fiber, 2.5 g Sugars, 12.5 g Protein;

LUNCH

GREEK FANTASY BOWL

 10 MINUTES    0 MINUTES    4 SERVINGS

INGREDIENTS

- 1 medium yellow bell pepper, cored, chopped
- 6 tablespoons hemp hearts
- 6 tablespoons chopped red onion
- 1 medium red bell peppers, cored, chopped
- 1/2 cup chopped artichokes
- 2 tablespoons chopped parsley leaves
- 14 cherry tomatoes, chopped
- 4 medium zucchini
- 2 tablespoons chopped mint
- 1 English cucumber
- For the Greek Dressing:
- 1/4 teaspoon dried oregano
- 1 tablespoon olive oil
- 1/2 teaspoon salt
- 2 teaspoons Italian seasoning
- 3 tablespoons red wine vinegar

HOW TO MAKE IT

1. Prepare the courgette and cucumber noodles. Cut them into spirals with a spiraliser or vegetable peeler and then distribute them evenly among four bowls.

2. Layer the courgette and cucumber noodles with artichokes, tomatoes, peppers, hemp hearts, onions, parsley and mint and put aside until ready to use.

3. Make the dressing. Take a small bowl, add all the ingredients for the dressing and mix them together.

4. Add the prepared dressing evenly to each bowl, swirl until the vegetables are thoroughly coated with the dressing and serve.

NUTRITION   250 Cal 14 g Fat, 3 g Saturated Fat 19 g Carbohydrates 5 g Fiber, 9 g Sugars, 13 g Protein;

CHICKPEA BONANZA SALAD BITES

 15 MINUTES  0 MINUTES  4 SERVINGS

INGREDIENTS

For the Bread:

- 1/2 teaspoon smoked paprika
- 1 1/2 cups crumbled rye bread, gluten-free
- 1 teaspoon garlic powder
- 2 tablespoons chopped parsley
- 1 small green chili pepper
- 2 tablespoons balsamic vinegar
- 1/2 teaspoon salt
- 1/3 teaspoon ground black pepper
- 1/2 tablespoon maple syrup
- 1/2 teaspoon cayenne pepper
- 1/3 cup of raisins

For the Salad:

- 2 scallions, chopped
- 1 teaspoon mustard paste
- 1/4 teaspoon ground black pepper
- 1/3 cup coconut yogurt
- 1/2 teaspoon salt
- 1/2 teaspoon minced garlic
- 1 tablespoons poppy seeds
- 1/3 cup chopped pickles
- 1 1/2 cup cooked chickpeas
- 2 tablespoons chopped chives and more for topping
- 1 lemon, juiced

HOW TO MAKE IT

1. Start by making the bread marinade. Place all the bread ingredients in a food processor and pulse for 1 minute until they are just combined; avoid over-mixing.

2. Take a round cookie cutter, adding 2 tablespoons of the bread mixture, pushing it into the mould and gently lifting it out.

3. Get the salad ready. Take a large bowl, add the chickpeas, chives, spring onions, pickles and garlic and crush the chickpeas with a fork until they are chopped.

4. Next, add the rest of the ingredients for the salad and mix until everything is well combined.

5. Put the bites together. To do this, generously cover each prepared bread bite with the preparation salad, scatter with chives and poppy seeds and then serve.

NUTRITION 210 Cal, 4 g Fat, 1 g Saturated Fat, 36 g Carbohydrates, 6 g Fiber, 4 g Sugars, 7 g Protein;

LUNCH
AVOCADO & CHICKPEAS SUMMER CUPS

 10 MINUTES    0 MINUTES    4 SERVINGS

INGREDIENTS

- 1 tablespoon minced shallots
- 2 1/2 tablespoons olive oil
- 1/3 teaspoon ground black pepper
- 1 tablespoon Dijon mustard
- 1 lime, zested, juiced
- 1 tablespoon apple cider vinegar
- 1/2 cup cucumber, diced
- 2 tablespoons chopped cilantro and more for topping
- 2 small avocados, peeled, pitted, diced
- 8 ounces hearts of palm
- 2 cups mixed greens
- 3/4 cup cooked chickpeas
- 2/3 teaspoon salt

HOW TO MAKE IT

1. In a medium-sized bowl, add the shallots and coriander, salt, black pepper, mustard, vinegar, lime juice and zest until well combined, then slowly stir in the olive oil until well mixed.

2. Then add the cucumber, hearts of palm and chickpeas, mix, stir in the avocado and then add some more coriander on top.

3. Distribute the mixed greens on four plates, top with the chickpea topping and then serve.

NUTRITION
280 Cal | 12.6 g Fat | 1.5 g Saturated Fat | 32.8 g Carbohydrates | 9.3 g Fiber | 1.2 g Sugars | 7.6 g Protein

LUNCH

PUMPKIN & MUSHROOM RISOTTO

 5 MINUTES   20 MINUTES   4 SERVINGS

INGREDIENTS

- 1/2 of a medium white onion, peeled, diced
- 1 rib of celery, diced
- 1/2 cup mushrooms
- 1 cup Brown rice
- 1/3 teaspoon ground black pepper
- 1/2 teaspoon salt
- 1/2 cup cooked and chopped pumpkin
- 1/2 teaspoon minced garlic
- 1/2 tablespoon coconut butter
- 2 cups vegetable stock
- 1 tablespoon olive oil
- 1 cup pumpkin puree

HOW TO MAKE IT

1. Get a medium saucepan, put it on medium heat, add oil and when it is hot, put in onions and celery, stir in the garlic and cook for 3 minutes until the onions start to soften.

2. Next, add mushrooms, salt and black pepper to taste and cook for 5 minutes.

3. Pour in the rice, stir in the pumpkin puree, then gradually pour in the stock till the rice has absorbed all the liquid and has softened.

4. Put in the butter, take the pan off the heat, mix until you have a creamy mixture and then serve.

Nutrition   218.5 Cal | 5.2 g Fat | 1.5 g Saturated Fat | 32.3 g Carbohydrates | 1.3 g Fiber - 3.8 g Sugars - 6.3 g Protein;

LUNCH

44

SWEET ENERGY POTATO SUSHI

 90 MINUTES    35 MINUTES   3 SERVINGS

INGREDIENTS

- 3/4 cup dry sushi rice
- 1 tbsp. agave nectar
- 1 tbsp. Tamari
- 1 14-oz. package silken tofu, drained
- 1 cup water
- 3 nori sheets
- 1 tbsp. rice vinegar
- 1 large sweet potato, peeled
- 1 medium avocado, pitted, peeled, sliced

HOW TO MAKE IT

1. Heat the oven to 400°F / 200°C.

2. In a small bowl, stir together the tamari sauce and agave syrup until well mixed and set aside.

3. Slice the sweet potato into large sticks about 1/2 inch thick. Lay them on a baking sheet covered with parchment paper and brush them with the tamari-agave mixture.

4. Cook in the oven until the sweet potatoes are tender - about 25 minutes - being sure to flip them halfway through so that the sides cook evenly.

5. While this is going on, bring the sushi rice, water and vinegar to the boil in a medium saucepan over a medium heat and cook for about 10 minutes until the liquid has all evaporated.

6. Whilst the rice is cooking, cut the block of tofu into long sticks. The sticks look like long, thin fries. Put to one side.

7. Take the pot off the heat and let the rice sit for 10-15 minutes.

8. Blanket your work surface with a piece of parchment paper, wash your hands, wet your fingers and place a nori sheet on the parchment paper.

9. While frequently moistening your hands, cover the nori sheet with a thin layer of sushi rice. Leave enough space to roll up the sheet.

10. Lay the roasted sweet potato strips in a straight line across the width of the sheet, about half an inch from the edge closest to you.

11. Place the tofu and avocado slices right next to the potato sticks and using the parchment paper as a guide, roll up the nori sheet into a tight cylinder.

12. Slice the cylinder into 8 equal pieces and place in the fridge. Again, repeat the process for the remaining nori sheets and fillings.

13. Serve the sushi chilled, or save it to enjoy later!

NUTRITION   Calories 467, Total Fat 17.1g, Carbohydrate 64g, Total Sugars 11g, Protein 15.4g

LUNCH

CLASSIC VEGAN BURRITOS

 10 MINUTES    20 MINUTES    6 SERVINGS

INGREDIENTS

- 2 cups chopped spinach
- 1/2 cup tomato salsa
- 6 tortillas, corn
- warm Guacamole as needed for serving
- 2 cups cooked rice
- 1 tablespoon olive oil
- 32 ounces refried beans

HOW TO MAKE IT

1. Turn on the oven, then set it to 375 degrees F and let it preheat.
2. Get a medium saucepan, set it to medium heat, include the beans and cook them for 3 to 5 minutes until they are soft, take the saucepan off the heat.
3. Lay a tortilla on a clean work surface, spread some of the beans into a log, leaving 2 inches of border, top with spinach, rice and salsa, then tightly wrap the tortilla to seal the filling like a burrito.
4. Again, repeat the process with the remaining tortillas, lay these burritos on a baking tray, brush with olive oil and then cook for 15 minutes until golden brown.
5. Then serve the burritos with guacamole.

NUTRITION   421 Cal, 9 g Fat, 2 g Saturated Fat, 70 g Carbohydrates, 11 g Fiber, 3 g Sugars, 15 g Protein

46

BURGERS

Burgers

PUMPKIN BURGERS

 10 MINUTES    3 MINUTES    2 SERVINGS

INGREDIENTS

- 1 teaspoon turmeric
- 1 tablespoon flax meal
- 3 tablespoons hot water
- 1 tablespoon pumpkin powder
- 3 tablespoon pumpkin puree
- 2 tablespoons breadcrumbs
- 2 hamburger buns
- 1/2 teaspoon chili flakes
- 1 tablespoon pumpkin seeds

HOW TO MAKE IT

1. Blend the flax flour and hot water in the mixing bowl. Beat the mixture and add pumpkin powder, pumpkin puree, breadcrumbs, chilli flakes and turmeric.

2. Whisk the mixture together. Mix in the pumpkin seeds.

3. Shape 2 burgers with the help of the burger mould.

4. Place the patties on top of your hot pan, close the lid and cook for 5 minutes turning to the other side halfway through.

5. Stuff the burger buns with the pumpkin burgers.

NUTRITION   Calories: 197, Fat: 5.6, Fiber: 3.3, Carbs: 30.5, Protein: 7.2

BURGERS

BALSAMIC BEET BURGER

 20 MINUTES    21 MINUTES   6 SERVINGS

INGREDIENTS

- 1 tbsp. balsamic vinegar
- 1 tsp. fresh parsley, chopped
- 1/4 tsp pepper
- 2 tbsp. olive oil
- 1 cup dry chickpeas
- 6 buns or wraps of choice
- 2 cups spinach, fresh or frozen, washed and dried
- 1/2 cup dry quinoa
- 2 tsp. onion powder
- 2 large beets
- 1/4 tsp Salt
- 2 tbsp. garlic powder

HOW TO MAKE IT

1. Preheat the oven to 400°F.
2. Pare and dice the beetroot into 1/4 inch or smaller cubes, put them in a bowl and coat the cubes with 1 tablespoon of olive oil and the onion powder.
3. Distribute the beet cubes on a baking tray and place the tray in the oven.
4. Fry the beetroots until they have softened, about 10-15 minutes. Remove them and set aside to allow the beets to cool.
5. Once the beets have cooled, place them in a food processor and add the cooked chickpeas and quinoa, vinegar, garlic, parsley and a pinch of pepper and salt.
6. Process until everything is crumbly, about 30 seconds.
7. Form the mixture into 6 equal-sized patties with the palms of your hands and place them in a small pan.
8. Set them in the freezer for up to 1 hour, until the patties feel firm to the touch.
9. In a frying pan, heat the remaining 1 tablespoon of olive oil over medium-high heat and add the patties.
10. Pan fry until browned on each side, about 4-6 minutes per side.
11. Stock or serve the burgers with a handful of spinach and, if desired, on the underside of the optional bun.
12. Garnish the burger with the sauce of your choice.

Nutrition Calories 353, Total Fat 9.2g, Saturated Fat 1.5g, Total Carbohydrate 57.8g, Total Sugars 9.2g, Protein 13.9g,

BLACK BEANS BURGER

 10 MINUTES   35 MINUTES   2 SERVINGS

INGREDIENTS

- Filling
- 1 Tablespoon. lime juice
- 2 teaspoon. chili powder
- Sea salt and freshly ground black pepper, to taste
- 1/2 cup quick cooking rolled oats
- 2 cups no-salt-added canned black beans, drained
- and liquid reserved
- 1 medium onion, quartered
- Buns
- 2 red onion slices, separated
- Condiments of your choosing (see headnote)
- 1 tomato, sliced
- 4 100% aots hamburger buns, split and toasted
- 4 leaves leaf lettuce

HOW TO MAKE IT

1. Process the first 5 ingredients in a food processor: (except for the chilli powder).
2. Put a lid on; mix until the mixture is chunky but not pureed.
3. The mixture should now be moist. Flavour with salt and pepper.
4. Spread some olive oil on your hands, this will prevent the mixture to stick on your hands. Grab two or three scoops of the mixture and shape 4 3 1/2-inch patties. Put in the fridge for 20 minutes.
5. Cook the burgers in a large skillet over medium heat for 10 minutes until lightly browned and cooked through, turning once.
6. Put the burgers on the hamburger buns with the lettuce, tomato and onion slices. Place on a plate and serve!

Nutrition   Calories: 430 | Fat: 14g | Carbs: 5g | Protein: 15g

COCO-CAULIFLOWER BURGERS

15 MINUTES   7 MINUTES   2 SERVINGS

INGREDIENTS

- 1 tablespoon coconut yogurt
- 1/2 cup water, for cooking
- 1 tablespoon breadcrumbs
- 1 teaspoon salt
- 7 oz cauliflower rice
- 1 teaspoon white pepper
- 1/4 cup mashed potato
- 1 tablespoon almond flour

HOW TO MAKE IT

1. Combine the cauliflower rice and mashed potatoes in the mixing bowl.
2. Include almond flour, salt, white pepper and coconut yoghurt.
3. Then wear gloves or grease your hands and shape the mixture into medium-sized patties.
4. Dust each patty with breadcrumbs and wrap in foil.
5. Fill the bowl of the Instant Pot with water and insert the steamer insert. Arrange the wrapped burgers on the steamer insert and close the lid.
6. Boil the patties for 7 minutes on a high setting (manual mode). Then let the natural pressure release for 10 minutes. Serve.
7. Alternatively you can also use a regular steamer and cook the patties for 10 minutes.

NUTRITION   Calories: 163, Fat: 9, Fibre: 4.8, Carbs: 17, Protein: 6.6

SIMPLE SWEET POTATO BURGERS

10 MINUTES   20 MINUTES   2 SERVINGS

INGREDIENTS

- 1/2 cup kale
- 1/2 cup water, for cooking
- 1 teaspoon chives
- 1 teaspoon olive oil
- 1/2 teaspoon salt
- 1/2 onion, diced
- 1 sweet potato
- 1 teaspoon cayenne pepper
- 3 tablespoon flax meal

HOW TO MAKE IT

1. Grab a steamer and pour some water in it.
2. Put the sweet potato on the steamer insert and close the lid, cook for 15 minutes. You can also easily boil the potatoes in a pot until they result soft.
3. Add the onion, chives and kale to the blender in the meantime. Blend until everything is smooth.
4. Add the pureed mixture to the mixing bowl.
5. Once the sweet potato is cooked, halve it and add all the flesh to the kale mixture. Gently mix it through with the help of a fork.
6. Next, add the flax meal, salt and cayenne pepper. Mix well.
7. Shape into medium burgers with the help of your fingertips.
8. Pre-heat a sauce pan and sauté the oil for 2 minutes.
9. Place the patties and fry them for 2 minutes on each side.

NUTRITION Calories: 139, Fat: 6.4, Fiber: 6, Carbs: 19.7, Protein: 4.3

BURGERS
PAPRIKA & ALMOND BUTTER POTATO PATTIES

 10 MINUTES    15 MINUTES    4 SERVINGS

INGREDIENTS

- 1/2 teaspoon smoked paprika
- 2 tablespoon corn flour
- 1/4 teaspoon chili flakes
- 1/2 teaspoon salt
- 3 russet potatoes, peeled
- 1 teaspoon almond butter
- 3 tablespoon aquafaba

HOW TO MAKE IT

1. Whisk the aquafaba using a hand mixer until you get soft peaks.
2. Grate all three potatoes finely and add them to aquafaba in the mixing bowl, whisk well.
3. Season with salt, smoked paprika, chilli flakes and flour. Stir carefully.
4. Grab a sauce pan, pour 1 tablespoon pf almond butter and let it melt.
5. Then form medium sized patties with the help of the spoon; squeeze them a little with the palms of your hands and place them in the hot almond butter.
6. Roast the patties for 3 minutes and then turn them to the other side. Roast the patties for a further 4 minutes. Serve warm.

NUTRITION
Calories: 150, Fat: 2.5, Fiber: 4.4, Carbs: 29, Protein: 4

BURGERS

LENTIL & CARROT BURGERS

20 MINUTES   26 MINUTES   7 SERVINGS

INGREDIENTS

- 4 tablespoon oat flour
- 1 teaspoon olive oil
- 1/2 carrot, peeled
- 1 tablespoon dried dill
- 1 teaspoon salt
- 1 cup lentils, soaked overnight
- 1 teaspoon cayenne pepper
- 1 cup of water

HOW TO MAKE IT

1. Place the lentils in a pot with the water, carrot, salt and cayenne pepper.
2. Shut the lid and boil the ingredients for 25 minutes.
3. Place the cooked ingredients in the blender and mix until smooth.
4. Add the flour and the dried dill. Mix everything until it is smooth. If the mixture is liquid - just add more flour.
5. Shape the burgers and place them on a no stick pan. Let them cook until brownish flipping the patties on the other side halfway through.
6. Serve warm.

NUTRITION   Calories 122, Fat 1.1, Fiber 8.7, Carbs 20.7, Protein 7.7

TUMERIC BEANS BURGER

 15 MINUTES    5 MINUTES    5 SERVINGS

INGREDIENTS

- 1 tablespoon fresh parsley, chopped
- 1/2 cup of water
- 1 teaspoon salt
- 1/4 cup sweet corn, cooked
- 1 cup ground chicken (vegan: 1 cup black beans, cooked)
- 1/2 yellow sweet pepper, chopped
- 1 teaspoon turmeric
- 2 tablespoons oat bread crumbs

HOW TO MAKE IT

1. Puree the black beans until you get a puree and mix it with salt, corn, turmeric, parsley and sweet pepper. (Or mix the chicken as it comes).
2. Carefully mix with the help of a spoon.
3. Pour in the breadcrumbs and give it another stir.
4. Form the burgers from the black bean mixture and freeze for 30 minutes.
5. Then cover each burger in foil and place them on your steamer insert where you previously boiled some water.
6. Shut the lid and cook for 15 minutes.
7. Take the foil off the burgers and garnish them on the plate with salad leaves and other topping of your choice.

NUTRITION   Calories: 155, Fat: 0.9, Fiber: 6.5, Carbs: 28.8, Protein: 9.2

MUSHROOM SALMON SPICY BURGER

🧤 10 MINUTES 🍴 14 MINUTES 🍽 4 SERVINGS

INGREDIENTS

- 1/2 teaspoon chili flakes
- 1 teaspoon dried dill
- 1/2 teaspoon olive oil
- 1 salmon fillet (vegan:1/2 cup silken tofu)
- 1 tablespoon dried parsley
- 1/2 teaspoon salt
- 3 tablespoon flax meal
- 2 cups mushrooms, chopped
- 1 onion, diced

HOW TO MAKE IT

1. Place the chopped mushrooms in the blender. Blend well.
2. Take a sauce pan and add the mixture with the onion and olive oil.
3. Gently stir and close the lid. Cook for 10 minutes.
4. Meanwhile, blend the salmon in a food processor. Mix it with salt, chilli flakes, dried parsley and dried dill. Then add flaxseed meal and pulse for 10 seconds. (Vegan:Mash the tofu in a food processor)
5. Once the mushroom mixture is cooked, add it to the bowl and combine with the salmon. Mix well.
6. Assemble the patties.
7. Preheat your oven to 400F. Lightly grease a baking tray or use parchment paper and place the burgers on top nicely . Cook for 12-15 minutes. Remove from the oven and let them cool down a bit.
8. Serve warm.

NUTRITION Calories: 47, Fat: 2.6, Fiber: 2.5, Carbs: 5.4, Protein: 2.6

BURGERS

SOY AND MUSTARD SEITAN BURGERS

 10 MINUTES    2 MINUTES   1 SERVINGS

INGREDIENTS

- 1 seitan steak
- 1 tablespoon apple cider vinegar
- 1 teaspoon soy sauce
- 1 burger bun
- 1 teaspoon mustard
- 1 teaspoon olive oil
- 1 teaspoon onion powder

HOW TO MAKE IT

1. Prepare the sauce for seitan steak: Stir together the soy sauce, onion powder, olive oil and apple cider vinegar.

2. Brush each side of the seitan steak with the sauce and place in the Instant Pot.

3. Cover the lid and cook in manual mode (high pressure) for 2 minutes (quick release of pressure).

4. In the meantime, cut the burger buns in half and spread with mustard.

5. Put the seitan steak on one half of the burger bun and top with the second half.

NUTRITION   Calories: 303, Fat: 8.8, Fiber: 2.8, Carbs: 24.9, Protein: 26.8

Burgers

SPINACH FLAX MEAL BURGERS

10 MINUTES   10 MINUTES   7 SERVINGS

INGREDIENTS

- 1 teaspoon olive oil
- 1 tablespoon coconut yogurt
- 4 tablespoon panko breadcrumbs
- 2 tablespoon flax meal
- 3 cups spinach, chopped
- 1/2 teaspoon chili flakes
- 1 teaspoon salt
- 6 tablespoon hot water
- 2 tablespoon coconut shreds

HOW TO MAKE IT

1. Together in the mixing bowl, combine flax meal and hot water. Whisk the mixture together.
2. Then include shredded coconut, panko breadcrumbs, spinach, chilli flakes, coconut yoghurt and salt.
3. Stir the mixture until it is homogeneous.
4. Brush the inside of a no stick pan with olive oil.
5. Shape patties from the spinach mixture with the help of 2 spoons and transfer them to the pan.
6. Roast them for 5/10 minutes. You can flip the patties during cooking if desired.

NUTRITION   Calories: 47, Fat: 2.9, Fiber: 1.3, Carbs: 4.5, Protein: 1.5

TEMPEH & BLACK BEANS PATTIES

 15 MINUTES    11 MINUTES    5 SERVINGS

INGREDIENTS

- 1/2 teaspoon salt
- 1 carrot, peeled
- 1 teaspoon golden syrup
- 1/4 teaspoon minced garlic
- 1/2 cup water, for cooking
- 10 oz tempeh
- 1 teaspoon onion powder
- 2 oz black beans, canned
- 1 tablespoon tomato sauce
- 4 tablespoon oatmeal

HOW TO MAKE IT

1. Dice the tempeh and place in a pan. Cover with water and bring to a boil. Shut the lid and simmer for 10 minutes.
2. While the tempeh is cooking, mince the carrot and place in the food processor.
3. Put in the chopped garlic, oatmeal onion powder, salt, canned beans, tomato sauce and golden syrup.
4. Blend the mixture for 2-3 minutes.
5. Then include the cooked tempeh and blend for 1 minute more. Make sure the final texture of the mixture is not too smooth.
6. Using the burger mould, shape the burgers. Refrigerate them until they are firm.
7. Preheat your oven to 400F. Lightly grease a baking tray or use parchment paper and place the burgers on top nicely. Cook for 12-15 minutes. Remove from the oven and let them cool down a bit.

NUTRITION Calories: 175, Fat: 6.6, Fiber: 2.5, Carbs: 18, Protein: 13.7

59

WRAPS

MINTY TANDORY BEEF WRAPS

 5 MINUTES  22 MINUTES  5 SERVINGS

INGREDIENTS

- 3 tablespoon Mint sauce
- 4 tablespoon Yogurt
- Sliced onions
- 2 tablespoon Tandoori curry paste
- 2 tablespoon Olive oil
- Quartered lime
- 8 Chapatis
- Shredded red cabbage head
- 600 g grass fed beef in cubes (vegan: 600 g Cubed tofu)
- Sliced garlic cloves

HOW TO MAKE IT

1. Let's start by taking a bowl and mixing the yogurt, cabbage and mint sauce, then set them aside.

2. Place the beef/tofu and the tandoori paste in a frying pan with a little oil. Next, fry the tofu a little on each side so that it turns golden brown. Remove it from the heat when you are done.

3. We can add the garlic and onions to the same pan next and cook them a little. Add the tofu again after ten minutes and continue to cook it a little more.

4. Warm the chapatis according to the instructions on the packet and then stuff them with the tandoori beef/tofu and the sauce you have prepared. Garnish with the lime quarters and serve.

NUTRITION Calories: 211 Carbs: 22g Fat: 7g Protein: 19g

WRAPS

HUMMUS AND OLIVE WRAP

🧤 6 MINUTES   🍳 5 MINUTES   🍴 6 SERVINGS

INGREDIENTS

- 2 Romaine lettuce leaves, for the wrapping
- 2 tablespoons kalamata olives, quartered
- Handful of baby spinach
- 1/4 cup crispy chickpeas
- 1/4 cup hummus
- 1/4 cup cherry tomatoes halved
- 2 tablespoons lemon juice, fresh

HOW TO MAKE IT

1. Grab a bowl and mix all ingredients: except hummus and salad leaves, mix well.
2. Spoon the hummus on top of the salad leaves and then top with the chickpea mixture.
3. Tuck in and serve.

NUTRITION   Calories: 55 Fat: 0g Carbohydrates: 12g Protein: 3g

WRAPS

MEDITERRANEAN VEGETABLE MIX WRAP

 15 MINUTES    0 MINUTES    4 SERVINGS

INGREDIENTS

- 4 tablespoon Kalamata Olives
- 1 grated Cucumber
- 7 oz. Plant-based Yogurt
- Corn Tortillas
- Pepper to Taste
- Salt to Taste
- 1/4 C., Diced Green Pepper
- 3 C. Chickpeas
- 1 Garlic Clove, Minced
- 2 cups Lettuce
- 2 tablespoon Lemon Juice
- 1/4 cup Onion diced
- 2 tablespoon Fresh Dill
- 1 Tomato, diced

HOW TO MAKE IT

1. Just before you start preparing this wrap, grate half of your cucumber into a mixing bowl.

2. Once this step is complete, lightly sprinkle the cucumber with salt to help get some of the excess water out.

3. When ready, you can now take your chickpeas and mash them well with a fork.

4. Take a bowl now and mix the cucumber, yoghurt, lemon juice, garlic and dill together. As soon as this is done, season with pepper and salt to your taste.

5. Once you are ready, spread out your wraps and layer the mashed chickpeas, lettuce and mixed vegetables. For added flavour, you can pour some tzatziki sauce on top before rolling up.

NUTRITION

Calories: 400, Carbs: 30g, Fats: 5g Proteins: 15g

SIMPLE LENTIL & TOMATO PASTE WRAP

10 MINUTES   30 MINUTES   4 SERVINGS

INGREDIENTS

- 1/3 cup Cilantro
- 1/3 cup Tomato Paste
- 2 tablespoon Olive Oil
- 2 cups Lentils
- Lentil flour Wraps
- 1 Onion diced
- 1 Garlic Clove minced

HOW TO MAKE IT

1. Start this recipe by taking a pot and place two cups of water and the lentils inside.

2. Heat everything to boiling before you turn down the temperature and simmer for ten minutes until the lentils are soft.

3. As soon as the lentils are cooked through, include the tomato paste, garlic and onion. Simmer all the ingredients together for another five minutes before switching off the heat and seasoning to taste.

4. Lastly, line your wraps, distribute the mixture in the centre and roll the wrap. It's ready, enjoy!

Nutrition Calories: 400 Carbs: 50g Fats: 5g Proteins: 20g

WRAPS

CILANDROLAMB WRAP WITH ALMOND SAUCE

 5 MINUTES　　 30 MINUTES　　 1 SERVINGS

INGREDIENTS

- 1/4 cup Cilantro
- Gluten free Wrap
- 1 teaspoon Olive Oil
- 1/3 Cucumber, diced
- 1 Garlic Cloves, minced
- 1 cup chopped lamb (vegan: Extra-firm Tofu 1 Cup, Diced)
- 1/3 cup carrots, shredded
- 1/4 cup Almond Sauce

HOW TO MAKE IT

1. To begin this recipe, grab a frying pan and place it over medium heat.
2. As it heats up, start adding your olive oil and begin cooking the lamb/tofu for about 15 minutes (5 minutes for the tofu).
3. Add the garlic after five minutes and cook for another minute. By this time, all the liquid should have disappeared from the tuna/tofu.
4. Take the pan off the heat and add the almond sauce. Give it a good stir so that the lamb/tofu pieces are evenly coated!
5. When you are ready to make your wraps, spread the lamb/tofu on your wrap, add the cubed and chopped vegetables on top and roll everything up nice and tight before serving.
6. For added flavour, you can add some fresh coriander!

NUTRITION　　Calories: 270 Carbs: 12g Fats: 15g Proteins: 20g

VEGAN BUFFALO WRAP

 5 MINUTES    15 MINUTES    4 SERVINGS

INGREDIENTS

- 1/2 teaspoon Dried Dill
- 8 tablespoon Almond Milk
- 1 1/2 tablespoon Apple Cider Vinegar
- 4 Gluten free Wraps
- 1 cup Tomatoes, diced
- 1 cup Cashews
- Salt to taste
- 1 teaspoon Olive Oil
- 2 cups Kale, Chopped
- Pepper (to Taste)
- 1/2 teaspoon Dried Parsley
- 1/2 Cup Buffalo Sauce
- 1 cup grass fed beef, chopped (vegan: 1 cup seitan, chopped)

HOW TO MAKE IT

1. Begin this recipe by blending together the almond milk, apple cider vinegar, cashews, pepper, salt, parsley and dill in a food processor.
2. Once done, put the sauce to one side.
3. Grab a saucepan and place it on a medium heat. As soon as it is warm, put in some olive oil and start cooking your beef cubes. Usually it takes around eight minutes. (same for seitan)
4. Once the beef is well cooked, start adding the buffalo sauce and cook for another minute.
5. Once these steps are completed, take a moment to mix the kale in a bowl with the olive oil and spices.
6. Lastly assemble your wrap. To do so, remove your wrap and distribute your ranch dressing over the top.
7. Once the dressing is applied, begin building up the wrap by layering the kale, tomato and beef pieces.
8. For the finishing touch, add some buffalo sauce on top and then start wrapping it up!

NUTRITION Calories: 250 Carbs: 25g Fats: 15g Proteins: 20g

WRAPS

SOY FLAVOURED RED CABBAGE WRAP

 10 MINUTES    0 MINUTES   4 SERVINGS

INGREDIENTS

- Red Cabbage (1 C., Shredded)
- Carrot (1 C., Chopped)
- Ground Ginger (1/4 t.)
- Seed Butter (1/2 C.)
- Garlic Powder (1 T.)
- Large Lettuce Leaves 4
- Lime Juice (2 T.)
- Red Pepper (1 C., Chopped)
- Soy Sauce (1 T.)
- Cucumber (1 C., Chopped)
- Olive Oil (1 T.)

HOW TO MAKE IT

1. To make the sauce, use a small bowl and combine the oil, garlic, soy sauce, juice of the lime, ground ginger, red pepper flakes and the seed butter.

2. When everything is well mixed, put it to one side.

3. Let's put together the wrap! Spread the lettuce leaves out flat and distribute the dressing over the top.

4. Pile all the vegetables and roll up. Enjoy your veggie-filled wrap!

NUTRITION   Calories: 250 Carbs: 15g Fats: 20g Proteins: 10g

WRAPS
BBQ SAUCE CHIKPEAS COLESLAW WRAP

🧤 10 MINUTES 🍳 0 MINUTES 🍴 4 SERVINGS

INGREDIENTS

- Chickpeas (2 C.)
- BBQ Sauce (1/2 C.)
- 4 Gluten-free Tortillas
- Coleslaw (2 C.)

HOW TO MAKE IT

1. Take a blender bowl and mix the BBQ with the chickpeas.
2. You can make this wrap in no time! First, pick up a mash bowl and mix the BBQ with the chickpeas.
3. Then lay out your tortillas and put the coleslaw and chickpeas in the middle.
4. To finish it off, then wrap the tortilla and microwave it for a few seconds to heat it up before enjoying!

Nutrition Calories: 450, Carbs: 50g, Fats: 5g, Proteins: 10g

CURRY MANGO TAHINI WRAPS

🧤 15 MINUTES　　🥄 0 MINUTES　　🍴 3 SERVINGS

INGREDIENTS

- 1 1/2 cups cooked chickpeas
- 1 red bell pepper, deseeded and diced
- 1 1/2 cups shredded lettuce
- 1/4 teaspoon sea salt (optional)
- 3 tablespoons tahini
- 3 to 4 tablespoons water
- 1/2 cup fresh cilantro, chopped
- 1 tablespoon curry powder
- 1 cup diced mango
- 3 large Gluten-free wraps
- Zest and juice of 1 lime

HOW TO MAKE IT

1. Blend together the tahini, curry powder, lime zest, lime juice and sea salt (if desired) in a large bowl until smooth and creamy. Whisk in 3 to 4 tablespoons of water to dilute the mixture.

2. Place the cooked chickpeas, mango, coriander and peppers in the bowl. Swirl the mixture until it is well covered.

3. Lay the wraps on a clean work surface. Divide the chickpea and mango mixture between the wraps. Scatter the shredded lettuce on top and tightly roll up.

4. Serve immediately.

NUTRITION　Calories: 436　Fat: 17.9g　Carbs: 8.9g　Protein: 15.2g　Fiber: 12.1g

EXOTIC TOFU LETTUCE WRAPPED

 2 MINUTES   15 MINUTES   4 SERVINGS

INGREDIENTS

- 1/2 pineapple, peeled, cored, cut into cubes
- 4 large lettuce leaves
- 1 tablespoon roasted sesame seeds
- 14-ounce Veal cut into 1/2-inch cubes (vegan: 14-ouce package extra firm tofu, drained and cut)
- 1/4 cup low-sodium soy sauce
- Salt and ground black pepper, to taste
- 1 small white onion, diced
- 1 garlic clove, minced
- 1 tablespoons coconut sugar (optional)
- 2 tablespoons sesame oil (optional)

HOW TO MAKE IT

1. In a bowl, combine the soy sauce, garlic, sesame oil (if desired) and coconut sugar. Give it a stir to mix them well.

2. Place the veal/tofu cubes in the bowl with the soy sauce mixture and press them to coat them well. Cover the bowl with plastic and put it in the fridge for a minimum of 2 hours to marinate.

3. Place the marinated veal/tofu in a saucepan and heat it up over a medium flame. Put the diced onion and pineapple into the pan and mix well.

4. Season with salt (if desired) and pepper and sauté for 15 minutes. The onions has to be lightly browned and the pineapple cubes soft.

5. Spread the lettuce leaves on 4 plates and then pour the veal/tofu-pineapple mixture on top.

6. Scatter with sesame seeds and serve immediately.

NUTRITION   Calories: 259 Fat: 15.4g Carbs: 20.5g Protein: 12.1g Fiber: 3.2g

WRAPS

PAPRIKA BLACK BEAN & QUINOA LETTUCE WRAP

 30 MINUTES    15 MINUTES    6 SERVINGS

INGREDIENTS

- 1 teaspoon salt (optional)
- 6 large lettuce leaves
- 1/2 onion, chopped
- 1/4 cup deseeded and chopped bell pepper
- 1/2 teaspoon red pepper flakes
- 2 tablespoons avocado oil (optional)
- 2 tablespoons minced garlic
- 1/2 teaspoon paprika
- 1/2 cup almond flour
- 1 teaspoon pepper (optional)
- 1/2 cup cooked quinoa
- 1 cup cooked black beans

HOW TO MAKE IT

1. In a frying pan, heat 1 tablespoon of the avocado oil (if desired) over medium-high heat.
2. Include the peppers, onions, garlic, salt (if desired) and pepper. Allow to sauté for 5 minutes or until the peppers are soft.
3. Switch off the heat and leave the vegetables to cool for 10 minutes, then put them in a food processor. Include the quinoa, beans and flour.
4. Add the paprika and red pepper flakes. Continue to combine until the mixture is thick and well mixed.
5. Cover a baking tray with parchment paper, then use your hands to shape the mixture into 6 patties and lay them on the baking tray.
6. Put the tin in the freezer for 5 minutes to set the patties.
7. In a frying pan, warm the remaining avocado oil (if desired) over a high heat.
8. Put the patties in and cook for 6 minutes or until well browned on both sides. Flip the patties halfway through.
9. Place the patties in the lettuce leaves and serve immediately.

NUTRITION   Calories: 200 Fat: 10.6g Carbs: 40.5g Protein: 9.5g Fiber: 8.2g

PASTA & NOODLES

71

PASTA

SIMPLE VEGETABLES NOODLES

 10 MINUTES   8 MINUTES   4 SERVINGS

INGREDIENTS

- 1 batch Stir Fry Sauce, prepared
- 4 garlic cloves, minced
- 2 tablespoons sesame oil
- 1 large onion, chopped
- 1 cup red bell pepper, chopped
- Salt and black pepper, to taste
- 2 cups soy noodles, cooked
- 1 cup mushrooms, chopped
- 1 cup broccoli, chopped

HOW TO MAKE IT

1. In a pan, heat the sesame oil over medium heat and throw the garlic, onions, peppers, broccoli and mushrooms.
2. Fry for about 5 minutes and include soy noodles, Stir fry sauce.
3. Blend well and cook for 3 minutes more. Serve on plates to enjoy.

NUTRITION   Calories: 567 Total Fat: 48g Total Carbs: 6g Fiber: 4g; Net Carbs: 2g Sodium: 373mg Protein: 33g

PASTA

SPICY VEGETABLES NOODLES WITH SIRIRACHA SAUCE

 10 MINUTES    7 MINUTES    2 SERVINGS

INGREDIENTS

- 2 nests of soy noodles
- 150g mushrooms, sliced
- 1 head of broccoli, cut into bite sized florets
- 1 courgette, halved
- 1 onion, finely sliced
- 1 tablespoon olive oil
- For Sauce
- 2 tablespoons boiled water
- 1 tablespoon almond butter
- 1 teaspoon Sriracha
- 3 tablespoons soy sauce
- 1/4 cup sweet chili sauce
- For Topping
- 2 teaspoons dried chili flakes

HOW TO MAKE IT

1. In a cooking pot, heat the olive oil over medium heat and add the onions.
2. Brown for about 2 minutes and add broccoli, courgettes and mushrooms.
3. Sauté for 5 minutes while stirring occasionally.
4. In a bowl, whisk together the sweet chilli sauce, soy sauce, Sriracha, water and almond butter.
5. Boil the noodles according to the packet instructions and put them in with the vegetables.
6. Mix in the sauce and garnish with the dried chilli flakes and sesame seeds to serve.

NUTRITION   Calories: 351 Total Fat: 27g Protein: 25g Total Carbs: 2g Fiber: 1g Net Carbs: 1g

PASTA

CLASSIC ASIAN NOODLES

 15 MINUTES    8 MINUTES    4 SERVINGS

INGREDIENTS

- 200 g courgettes, sliced
- 1 tablespoon agave syrup
- 1/2 bunch fresh coriander, chopped
- 4 tablespoons vegetable oil
- 2 garlic cloves, minced
- 300 g mixed oriental mushrooms, such as oyster, shiitake and enoki, cleaned and sliced
- 1 fresh red chili
- 2 limes, to serve
- 2 tablespoons low-salt soy sauce
- 1/2 tablespoon rice wine
- 100 g baby spinach, chopped Hot chili sauce, to serve
- 2 (1-inch) pieces of ginger
- 200 g thin brown rice noodles, cooked according to packet instructions and drained
- 6 spring onions, reserving the green part
- 1 teaspoon sesame oil
- 1 teaspoon corn flour

HOW TO MAKE IT

1. In a large wok, heat the sesame oil over a high heat and add the mushrooms.

2. Sauté for around 4 minutes and include the garlic, chilli, ginger, courgette, coriander stalks and the white part of the spring onions.

3. Fry for around 3 minutes until the mushrooms are soft and lightly golden.

4. While this is going on, combine the cornflour and 2 tablespoons of water in a bowl.

5. Pour the soy sauce, agave syrup, sesame oil and rice wine into the cornflour mixture.

6. Pour this mixture into the pan with the vegetable mixture and cook for around 3 minutes or until it thickens.

7. Include the spinach and noodles and stir everything together well. Mix in the coriander leaves and toss with lime wedges hot chilli sauce and serve with reserved spring onions.

NUTRITION   Calories: 314, Total Fat: 22g, Protein: 26g, Total Carbs: 3g, Fiber: 0.3g, Net Carbs: 2.7g

PASTA

BOK CHOY CUMIN RICE

 12 MINUTES   10-13MINUTES   4-6 SERVINGS

INGREDIENTS

- 1/2 teaspoon salt (optional)
- Water, as needed
- Two teaspoons ground cumin
- 12 baby bok choy heads, ends trimmed and sliced lengthwise
- 1-inch piece fresh ginger, grated
- 2 cups cooked brown rice
- Two tablespoons coconut oil (optional)
- 1 teaspoon ground turmeric
- One large onion, finely diced

HOW TO MAKE IT

1. In a large frying pan, heat the coconut oil (if desired) over medium heat.
2. Fry the onion for 5 minutes until translucent.
3. Whisk in the cumin, ginger, turmeric and salt (if desired). Cook and add the bok choy and stir-fry for 5 to 8 minutes, or until the bok choy is soft but still crunchy.
4. Pour in water 1 to 2 tablespoons at a time so the bok choy doesn't stick to the pan.
5. Arrange the dish over the brown rice.

NUTRITION calories: 447 fat: 8.9g carbs: 75.6g protein: 29.7g fiber: 19.1g

PASTA

RICH PUMPKIN SAUCE PASTA

15 MINUTES • 5 MINUTES • 6 SERVINGS

INGREDIENTS

- 12 ounces dried gluten-free penne pasta
- 3/4 teaspoon salt
- 1/4 teaspoon ground nutmeg
- 1 tablespoon fresh sage, chopped
- 1 cup almond milk, plus more as needed
- 3 garlic cloves
- 1 tablespoon olive oil
- 1 tablespoon lemon juice
- Fresh parsley, for garnish
- 1 cup raw cashews, soaked in water 4-8 hours, drained and rinsed
- 1 cup pumpkin puree, canned

HOW TO MAKE IT

1. In a large pot, boil salted water and add noodles.
2. Boil according to package instructions and pour the pasta into a colander.
3. Place the pasta in a large serving bowl and give it a dash of olive oil to keep it from sticking.
4. Place the pumpkin, cashews, milk, lemon juice, garlic, salt and nutmeg in a food processor and blend until smooth.
5. Mix the sauce and pour it over the pasta. Swirl to coat well.
6. Decorate with fresh parsley and serve hot.

NUTRITION Calories: 431 Total Fat: 31g Protein: 35g Total Carbs: 3g Fiber: 0.5g Net Carbs: 2.5g

PASTA

77

PASTA WITH PESTO SAUCE

 15 MINUTES    10 MINUTES   6 SERVINGS

INGREDIENTS

- 2 tablespoons lemon juice
- 2 tablespoons flour
- 1/2 cup Kalamata olives, halved
- 1/2 cup blue cheese, crumbled
- Red pepper flakes, to taste
- 1 tablespoon olive oil, plus a dash
- 1 celery stalk, thinly sliced
- 1/2 cup vegan pesto
- 6-ounces gluten-free pasta, dried
- 8 romaine lettuce leaves
- Salt and black pepper, to taste
- 1 cup fresh arugula, packed
- 1 cup full-Fat coconut milk
- 1 cup chickpeas, cooked
- 1 1/2 cups cherry tomatoes, halved
- 1/4 onion, finely chopped
- 1 cup almond milk, unflavored and unsweetened

HOW TO MAKE IT

1. Cook salted water in a large pot, adding the pasta, cook as per package instructions and drain in a colander.
2. Place the pasta into a large serving bowl and add a drizzle of olive oil to prevent sticking.
3. Put olive oil in a large saucepan over a medium heat and stir in the flour.
4. Let cook for around 4 minutes until the mixture starts to smell nutty. Pour in the coconut and almond milk and stir.
5. Simmer the sauce for around 1 minute and add chickpeas, olives and rocket.
6. Mix well and season with lemon juice, red pepper flakes and salt and black pepper to taste.
7. Serve on plates and keep hot until eating.

NUTRITION   Calories: 220 Total Fat: 10g Protein: 31g Total Carbs: 1.5g Fiber: 0.5g Net Carbs: 1g

PASTA

BAKED PASTA BOLOGNESE & CASHEW BESCIAMELLA

 1 HOUR 10 MINUTES  20 MINUTES   8 SERVINGS

INGREDIENTS

For the Pasta:

- 1 packet gluten free penne pasta
- For the Bolognese Sauce:
- 2 cups mushrooms, sliced Salt, to taste
- 1/2 lemon, squeezed
- 1/2 teaspoon salt
- 1/2 cup water
- 1 tablespoon soy sauce
- 1 onion, chopped
- 1 small can lentils
- Pepper, to taste

For the Cashew Cream:

- 1 cup raw cashews
- 1 tablespoon brown sugar 1/2 cup tomato paste
- 1 teaspoon garlic, crushed 1 tablespoon olive oil
- 2 tomatoes, chopped

For the White Sauce:

- Sea salt, as required
- 3 tablespoons vegan butter
- 2 tablespoons all-purpose flour 1/3 cup vegetable broth
- 1 teaspoon black pepper
- 1 teaspoon Dijon mustard
- 2 cups coconut milk
- 1/4 cup nutritional yeast

HOW TO MAKE IT

1. Get a pot and boil water, add pasta, boil according to manufacturer's directions and set aside.

2. Sauté onion and garlic, mushrooms in olive oil and stir in soy sauce.

3. Pour in tomato paste, lentils and canned tomatoes and simmer, bolognese sauce is ready. Flavour it with salt and black pepper.

4. Add the lemon juice, cashews, water and salt to the blender, blend for 2 minutes. Pour this into the prepared sauce and turn the noodles in it.

5. In a pot, melt the vegan butter, put in the flour and stir. Add vegetable stock and coconut milk and mix well.

6. Let cook for approx. 5 minutes, while stirring constantly, then take off the cooker.

7. Pour in Dijon mustard, nutritional yeast, black pepper and sea salt. Pre-heat the oven to 430 degrees F.

8. Grab a rectangular ovenproof dish, place the pasta and the Bolognese sauce in it.

9. Then pour the white sauce over it and bake for 20 to 25 minutes.

NUTRITION   Calories: 314 Total Fat: 20g Protein: 31g Total Carbs: 2.5g Fiber: 0.8g Net Carbs: 1.7g

PASTA

CHINESE VEGETABLES NOODLES

 10 MINUTES    20 MINUTES    4 SERVINGS

INGREDIENTS

- 1 red pepper, chopped in small cubes 1 can baby corn
- 2 tablespoons soy sauce
- 3 carrots, chopped
- 1/2 teaspoon curry powder Salt and black pepper, to taste
- 3 tablespoons sesame oil
- 1 teaspoon rice vinegar
- 1 clove garlic, chopped
- 1 small packet soy vermicelli
- 1 teaspoon ginger powder
- 1/2 cup peas

HOW TO MAKE IT

1. Get a bowl and add the ginger powder, vinegar, soy sauce, curry powder and a pinch of salt.
2. Boil the noodles as per instructions and drain them.
3. Preheat the sesame oil and fry the vegetables in it for 10 minutes on medium heat.
4. Pour in the noodles and continue to cook for a further 3 minutes. Take off the heat and plate up to enjoy.

NUTRITION Calories: 329 Total Fat: 25g Protein: 20g Total Carbs: 6g Fiber: 1g, Net Carbs: 5g

GINGER & ONION SOUP

 9 MINUTES  9 MINUTES  4 SERVINGS

INGREDIENTS

- 1 can each of diced tomatoes and peppers (or freshly Prepared)
- 6 cups of vegetable broth
- 3 cups of green onions, diced
- 2 cups of bok choy, chopped
- 1 tablespoon of cilantro, chopped
- 3 teaspoons of garlic, minced
- 3 tablespoons of carrot, grated
- 2 cups of mushrooms, sliced
- 3 teaspoons of fresh ginger, grated

HOW TO MAKE IT

1. Place the ingredients listed: (except spring onions, carrot) into a pot and come to a boil over medium-high heat.
2. Lower heat to medium-low and boil for 6 minutes.
3. Add in spring onions and carrot and boil for 2 minutes.
4. Scatter the coriander over and serve.

NUTRITION
Calories: 65 - Fat: 2g Carbohydrates: 5g Protein: 7g

BROCCOLI AVOCADO CREAM

 20 MINUTES 5 MINUTES  4 SERVINGS

INGREDIENTS

- Salt
- Pepper
- 2 cups broccoli florets, chopped
- 5 cups vegetable broth
- 2 avocados, chopped

HOW TO MAKE IT

1. Boil broccoli in boiling water for 5 minutes. Let drain well.
2. Place broccoli, vegetable broth, avocados, pepper and salt in mixer and blend until smooth.
3. Mix well and serve warm.

NUTRITION
Calories 265 Protein 35g Fat 13, Carbs 5

SOUPS

SWEET POTATOES & LEGUMES SOUP

 10 MINUTES   4 MINUTES   6 SERVINGS

INGREDIENTS

- 1 teaspoon turmeric, ground
- 6 cups veggie stock
- 1 cup lentils, dry
- 1 sweet potato, cubed
- Black pepper to the taste
- 30 ounces canned chickpeas, drained
- 1 teaspoon ginger powder
- 2 tablespoons mild curry powder
- A pinch of salt
- 15 ounces canned coconut milk

HOW TO MAKE IT

1. Add the chickpeas to your slow cooker. Include the lentils, sweet potato cubes, curry powder, ginger, turmeric, salt, pepper and broth.

2. Give it a stir and then combine with the coconut milk. Again stir, lid and simmer on high for 4 hours.

3. Scoop the chickpea soup out into bowls and serve. Enjoy!

NUTRITION   Calories: 302g, Fat: 22g, Carbs: 5g, Protein: 34g,

SPICY CURRY PUMPKIN SOUP

 25 MINUTES    25 MINUTES   4 SERVINGS

INGREDIENTS

- 1 tsp olive oil
- 1/2 tsp garlic, minced
- 1 1/2 tsp curry powder
- 1/2 tsp paprika
- 2 cups pumpkin, diced
- 1/2 cup tomato, chopped
- 1/2 cup onion, chopped
- 2 cups vegetable stock

HOW TO MAKE IT

1. Add the oil, garlic and onion to a pot and fry over moderate heat for 3 minutes.
2. Put the rest of the ingredients in the pot and heat to boiling.
3. Lower the heat and let it simmer, then cover and cook for 10 minutes.
4. Purée the soup with a hand mixer until smooth. Mix well and serve warm.

NUTRITION Calories: 340 Protein: 50 g Carbohydrate: 14 g Fat: 10g

GARLIC LEEK SOUP

 45 MINUTES   25 MINUTES   4 SERVINGS

INGREDIENTS

- 2 garlic clove, chopped
- 1 leek, sliced
- Salt to taste
- 1 shallot, sliced
- 1 onion, sliced
- 4 cups vegetable stock 1
- 1/2 tbsp olive oil

HOW TO MAKE IT

1. Place the stock and olive oil into a pan and heat to boiling. Pour in the remaining ingredients and mix well.
2. Put a lid on and let it simmer for 25 minutes.
3. Blend the soup with a hand blender until smooth.
4. Mix well and serve warm.

NUTRITION Calories 115, Protein 30g, Fat 0, Carbs 3

SOUPS

83

CREAMY COCONUT KALE SOUP

🧤 10 MINUTES   🥄 5 MINUTES   🍴 6 SERVINGS

INGREDIENTS

- 3 1/3 cup coconut milk
- 3 oz olive oil
- 1/4 tsp pepper
- 1 tsp salt
- 1 cup water
- 2 avocados
- 8 oz spinach
- 8 oz kale
- 1 fresh lime juice

HOW TO MAKE IT

1. In a pot, heat the olive oil at medium heat.
2. Put the kale and spinach in the pot and let them sauté for 2-3 minutes. Take the pot off the heat. Include the coconut milk, spices, avocado and water. Mix well.
3. Blend the soup with a hand blender until it is smooth and creamy.
4. Pour in the fresh lime juice and mix well. Serve and enjoy.

NUTRITION
Calories: 312 Protein: 9g Fat: 10 Carbs: 22

GARLIC BEET MEDLEY

 20 MINUTES  10 MINUTES  4 SERVINGS

INGREDIENTS

- 1 Cup Beets, Shredded
- 1/2 Teaspoon Onion Powder
- Dill for Garnish
- 2 Tablespoons Olive Oil
- 2 Tablespoons Lemon Juice, Fresh
- 1/2 Teaspoon Garlic Powder
- Sea Salt & Black Pepper to Taste
- 1/2 Cup Carrots, Shredded
- 2 Cups Cabbage, Shredded
- 3 Cups Vegetable Broth

HOW TO MAKE IT

1. Warm the oil in a pot and sauté all your vegetables with oil.
2. Add the broth and stir in the spices.
3. Let it simmer until cooked all the way through, and then add the dill.
4. Serve and enjoy!

NUTRITION
kcal: 263 Carbohydrates: 8 g Protein: 20.3 g Fat: 24 g

ITALIAN BASIL & TOMATO SOUP

 10 MINUTES  10 MINUTES   6 SERVINGS

INGREDIENTS

- 1 1/2 tsp kosher salt
- 1/2 tsp onion powder
- 1/4 tsp garlic powder
- 1/4 tsp dried basil leaves
- 1 tsp apple cider vinegar 2 tbsp erythritol
- 28 oz can tomatoes
- 2 cups water
- 1/4 cup basil pesto

HOW TO MAKE IT

1. Place tomatoes, garlic powder, onion powder, water and salt in a pot. Heat over medium heat and let it come to a boil. Lower the heat and let simmer for 2 minutes.
2. Take the pot off the heat and blend the soup with a hand mixer until it is smooth.
3. Whisk in the pesto, dried basil, vinegar and erythritol. Mix well and serve warm.

NUTRITION
kcal: 662 Carbohydrates: 18 g Protein: 8 g Fat: 55 g

SOUPS

SPICY PINEAPPLE & KALE MEDLY

 10 MINUTES  20 MINUTES  4 SERVINGS

INGREDIENTS

- 1/2 cup chopped cilantro
- 1 tbsp. hot pepper sauce or 1 tbsp. Tabasco sauce
- 2 minced garlic cloves
- 1/2 cup nuts butter
- 4 cups sliced kale
- 1 cup chopped onion
- 2 cups pineapple, undrained, canned & crushed
- 1 tbsp. vegetable oil

HOW TO MAKE IT

1. Fry the garlic and onions in the oil in a saucepan (preferably covered) until the onions are lightly browned, approximately 10 minutes, mixing often.

2. Rinse the kale until the onions are sautéed. Remove the stems from the kale. Mound the leaves on a chopping surface and cut them crosswise into slices (preferably 1" thick).

3. Next, add the pineapple and juice to the onions & let it all come to a boil. Mix in the kale, cover and simmer, stirring frequently, for about 5 minutes, until soft.

4. Mix in the hot pepper sauce and nuts butter and continue to simmer for a further 5 minutes.

5. Add salt to your taste.

NUTRITION kcal: 402 Carbohydrates: 7 g Protein: 21 g Fat: 34 g

SOUPS

AROMATIC BROCCOLI & MUSHROOM SOUP

 20 MINUTES  45 MINUTES  8 SERVINGS

INGREDIENTS

- 1/4 cup finely slashed onion
- 1 container (32 ounces) vegetable juices
- 2 cups of water
- 2 tablespoons lemon juice
- 1 bundle broccoli (around 1-1/2 pounds)
- 1 tablespoon olive oil
- 2 celery ribs, finely slashed
- 1 garlic clove, minced
- 1/2 pound cut crisp mushrooms
- 1 tablespoon diminished sodium soy sauce
- 2 medium carrots, finely slashed
- Rosmary to taste

HOW TO MAKE IT

1. Chop the broccoli florets into smaller pieces. Remove stems and chop.

2. Heat oil in a large saucepan over medium-high heat; fry mushrooms with rosemary until tender, 4-6 minutes. Whisk in soy sauce; take out of pan.

3. Mix broccoli stems, carrots, celery, onion, garlic, soup and water in same pot; cook until boiling. Lower heat; stew until vegetables are tender, 25-30 minutes.

4. Blend the soup with a hand blender and transfer back to the bowl.

5. Whisk in florets and mushrooms; bring to a simmer. Lower heat to medium; simmer until broccoli is tender, 8-10 minutes, tossing occasionally. Mix in lemon juice.

NUTRITION   kcal: 830 Carbohydrates: 8 g Protein: 45 g Fat: 64 g

SOUPS
TUMERIC CAULIFLOWER PAKORA CREAM

 20 MINUTES  20 MINUTES  8 SERVINGS

INGREDIENTS

- 1 teaspoon ground coriander
- 1 teaspoon ground turmeric
- 4 medium carrots, stripped and diced
- 2 celery ribs, diced
- 1 container (32 ounces) vegetable stock
- 1 teaspoon garam masala
- 1 teaspoon garlic powder
- 1 huge onion, diced
- 1 teaspoon ground cumin
- 1 huge head cauliflower, cut into little florets
- 5 medium potatoes, stripped and diced
- Lime wedges, discretionary
- 1 teaspoon salt
- 1 teaspoon pepper
- New cilantro leaves
- 1/2 teaspoon squashed red pepper chips Water or extra vegetable stock

HOW TO MAKE IT

1. Heat the first 14 ingredients to boiling point in a cooking pot on medium heat. Boil and agitate until the vegetables are tender, around 20 minutes.

2. Take off the cooker; leave to cool slightly. Blend in batches in a blender or food processor until smooth. Change consistency with added water (or additional broth) as desired.

3. Top with fresh coriander. Serve hot, with lime wedges if desired.

4. Alternative: Allow cooled soup to set in cooling compartments before adding cilantro. When ready to use, allow to partially thaw in the refrigerator compartment.

5. Warm up in a pan, mixing occasionally and increasing a little water if needed. Top with coriander. If desired, serve with lime wedges.

NUTRITION
kcal: 248 Carbohydrates: 7 g Protein: 1 g Fat: 19 g

GRANNY HERBS VEGGIES SOUP

 20 MINUTES    30 MINUTES   8 SERVINGS

INGREDIENTS

- 1 medium yellow summer squash, split and cut
- 1/4 teaspoon dill weed
- 1/2 teaspoon paprika
- 2 huge carrots, cut
- 1/4 teaspoon pepper
- 2 tablespoons olive oil
- 2 cups of water
- 1 medium zucchini, split and cut
- 1 can (14-1/2 ounces) diced tomatoes in sauce
- 1-1/2 cups vegetable soup
- 1-1/2 teaspoons garlic powder
- 2 medium onions, hacked
- 1/2 teaspoon salt
- 1 pound red potatoes (around 3 medium), cubed
- 1 teaspoon dried basil

HOW TO MAKE IT

1. Place oil in a large frying pan and heat over moderate heat. Put in onions and carrots; boil and stir until onions are tender, 4-6 minutes.

2. Include potatoes and boil for 2 minutes. Whisk in water, tomatoes, juice and spices.

3. Bring to boiling point. Lower heat; sauté, tossing, until potatoes and carrots are done and tender, 9 minutes.

4. Add yellow squash and courgette; simmer until vegetables are soft, another 9 minutes.

5. When ready to serve, or when desired, blend with extra broth until the desired consistency is achieved.

NUTRITION   kcal: 252 Carbohydrates: 12 g Protein: 1 g Fat: 11 g

89

SIDES

SIDES

GRILLED CORN WITH VEGANAISE COATING

 10 MINUTES    15 MINUTES    4 SERVINGS

INGREDIENTS

- 1 teaspoon lemon juice
- 1/2 cup gluten-free breadcrumbs
- 1 small handful cilantro
- 2 corn cobs
- 1/3 cup Veganaise

NUTRITION

Calories: 253 Total Fat: 13g Protein: 31g
Total Carbs: 3g Fiber: 0g Net Carbs: 3g

HOW TO MAKE IT

1. Heat the gas barbecue on high.
2. Place the corn on the grill and keep grilling until it is a golden brown on all sides.
3. Combine the vegenaise, coriander, breadcrumbs and lemon juice in a bowl.
4. Place the grilled corn on the cob with the breadcrumb coating.
5. Mix well and serve.

MARINATED RATATOUILLE SKEWERS

 10 MINUTES    20 MINUTES   6 SERVINGS

INGREDIENTS

- 1/2 red onion, diced
- 1/2 red capsicum, diced
- 8 button mushrooms, diced
- 3 tablespoons balsamic vinegar
- 1 small eggplant, diced
- 1 zucchini, diced
- 2 tablespoons extra virgin olive oil
- 2 tomatoes, diced
- 1 teaspoon dried thyme leaves
- 3 tablespoons soy sauce

HOW TO MAKE IT

1. Combine the vegetables in a large bowl with the soy sauce, olive oil, thyme and balsamic vinegar.
2. Fill the wooden skewers with the vegetables alternating them. Reserve the remaining marinade.
3. Place the skewers in the fridge to marinate for 1 hour. Prepare the barbecue over a medium heat.
4. Grill the marinated skewers on the grill for 5 minutes per side. Pour over the reserved marinade. Serve fresh.

NUTRITION

Calories: 166 Total Fat: 17g Carbs: 5g Net Carbs: 3g
Fiber: 1g Protein: 1g

SIDES

CREAMY CARROTS SALAD WITH CHICKPEAS

 10 MINUTES    10 MINUTES   8 SERVINGS

INGREDIENTS

- 1/2 cup of water
- 14 oz canned chickpeas
- 1/2 teaspoon salt
- 1 1/2 teaspoon salt
- Ground black pepper, to taste
- Carrots
- 1/2 cup vegan cream
- 1 teaspoon dried thyme
- 2 teaspoon paprika powder
- 1 teaspoon apple cider vinegar
- A big handful of lettuce
- 1 tablespoon oil
- 3 medium pickles
- 1 small onion
- 8 large carrots
- 1/2 teaspoon dried oregano
- 1 teaspoon dried oregano
- 1 1/2 tablespoon soy sauce
- Chickpea Salad

HOW TO MAKE IT

1. Place the carrots in a bowl with all the ingredients.
2. String a carrot onto a stick and arrange it on a plate.
3. Heat the barbecue on a high heat.
4. Cook the carrots on the grill for 2 minutes per side.
5. In a large salad bowl, mix the ingredients for the salad. Chill and serve!

NUTRITION   Calories: 661 Total Fat: 68g Carbs: 17g Net Carbs: 7g Fiber: 2g Protein: 4g

SIDES

BALSAMIC OVEN BAKED BRUSSELS SPROUTS

 10 MINUTES   40 MINUTES   4 SERVINGS

INGREDIENTS

- 1/2 teaspoon salt
- 1/4 teaspoon freshly ground black pepper
- 1 tablespoon balsamic vinegar
- 1/2 teaspoon dried rosemary
- 1-pound Brussels sprouts
- 2 teaspoons extra-virgin olive
- 4 teaspoons minced garlic (about 4 cloves)
- 1 teaspoon dried oregano

HOW TO MAKE IT

1. Preheat the oven to 400° F. Lay out a baking tray with parchment paper. Slice and cut the Brussels sprouts in half. Put them in a large bowl. Toss well with olive oil, garlic, oregano, rosemary, salt and pepper.

2. Put them on the prepared baking tray. Roast for 35 to 40 minutes, shaking the pan occasionally to achieve even browning, until the Brussels sprouts are crispy on the outside and tender on the inside.

3. Take out of the oven and transfer to a large bowl.

4. Whisk in the balsamic vinegar and distribute well.

5. Divide the Brussels sprouts among 4 serving bowls. Let them cool before serving.

NUTRITION   Calories: 77 Fat: 3g Protein: 4g Carbohydrates: 12g Fiber: 5g Sugar: 3g Sodium: 320mg

SIDES

AROMATIC GARLIC BAKED MASHROOM

 10 MINUTES   24 MINUTES   4 SERVINGS

INGREDIENTS

- 3 tablespoons balsamic vinegar
- 1/2 tablespoon soy sauce
- 1 teaspoon dried thyme
- 1/2 teaspoon dried basil
- 1/2 tablespoon tomato paste
- 2 large, whole portobello mushrooms
- 1/2 cup vegetable broth
- 1 tablespoon mirin
- A dash of ground black pepper
- 1/2 small yellow onion, diced
- 1 tablespoon vegan butter
- 1 large garlic clove, minced

HOW TO MAKE IT

1. In a pot, melt the butter over medium heat and whisk in half of the stock.
2. Heat to a simmer, then include the garlic and onion. Let simmer for 8 minutes.
3. In a bowl, whisk together the remaining ingredients: apart from the mushrooms.
4. Place this mixture on top of the onions in the pan and blend well. Let this filling simmer and then take it off the cooker.
5. Carefully clean the mushroom caps inside and outside and distribute the filling over the mushrooms.
6. Lay the mushrooms on a baking tray and baste with the remaining sauce and stock.
7. Put foil over them and place them on the grill to smoke. Put a lid on the grill and grill for 16 minutes on indirect heat. Serve warm.

NUTRITION Calories 379 Total Fat 29.7 g Saturated Fat 18.6 g Cholesterol 141 mg Sodium 193 mg Total Carbs 23.7g Fiber 0.9 g Sugar 1.3 g Protein 5.2 g

SIDES

SOY SAUCE & SESAME SPINACH

 1 HR. 10 MINUTES    3 MINUTES    4 SERVINGS

INGREDIENTS

- 1/2 teaspoon golden caster sugar
- 8 ounces spinach, stem ends trimmed
- 1 garlic clove, grated
- 1/2 teaspoon rice vinegar
- 1/2 tablespoon soy sauce
- 1 tablespoon toasted sesame oil
- 1/2 teaspoon toasted sesame seeds, crushed

HOW TO MAKE IT

1. Grab a no stick pan, heat it up and sauté the spinach until wilted.
2. While the spinach are cooking, take a mixing bowl, whisk together the sesame seeds, vinegar, sesame seeds, soy sauce and black pepper.
3. Toss in the spinach and mix well. Put in the fridge for 1 hour. Serve.

NUTRITION
Calories 201 Total Fat 8.9 g Cholesterol 57 mg Sodium 340 mg Total Carbs 24.7 g Fiber 1.2 g Sugar 1.3 g Protein 15.3 g

CURRY COATED CARROTS

 5 MINUTES    15 MINUTES    6 SERVINGS

INGREDIENTS

- 2 tablespoons pure maple syrup
- sea salt
- freshly ground black pepper
- 1-pound carrots, peeled and thinly sliced
- 2 tablespoons olive oil
- juice of 1/2 lemon
- 2 tablespoons curry powder

HOW TO MAKE IT

1. Place the carrots in a big pot and cover them with water. Cook them over medium heat until they are tender, about 10 minutes. Let the carrots drain and put them back into the pot over a medium-low heat.
2. Whisk in the olive oil, curry powder, maple syrup and lemon juice. Simmer, whisking constantly, until reduced, approximately 5 minutes. Add salt and pepper and serve immediately.

NUTRITION
Calories: 171 Fat: 3g Protein: 4g Carbohydrates: 34g Fiber: 5g Sugar: 3g Sodium: 129mg

SIDES

PAPRIKA FAVOURED SWEET POTATOES

 5 MINUTES    30 MINUTES    4 SERVINGS

INGREDIENTS

- 1/2 teaspoon salt (optional)
- 1/2 teaspoon dried thyme
- 2 pounds sweet potatoes
- 2 teaspoons extra-virgin olive oil
- 1/2 teaspoon smoked paprika
- 1/2 teaspoon garlic powder
- 1/2 teaspoon dried oregano
- 1/2 teaspoon ground cayenne pepper

HOW TO MAKE IT

1. Pre-heat the oven to 400oF. Cover a baking tray with parchment paper.

2. Rinse the potatoes, dry them and chop them into 3/4 cm cubes. Place them in a large bowl and drizzle the olive oil on top of the potatoes.

3. Grab another mixing bowl, combine the cayenne, paprika, oregano, thyme and garlic powder together.

4. Scatter the spices on the potatoes and stir until the potatoes are thoroughly coated.

5. Distribute the potatoes on the prepared baking tray in a single layer. Sprinkle with the salt (if using). Bake for 30 minutes, turning the potatoes after 15 minutes.

6. Evenly divide the potatoes between 4 portion containers. Leave to cool down completely before closing.

NUTRITION
Calories: 219 Fat: 3g Protein: 4g Carbohydrates: 46g Fiber: 7g Sugar: 9g Sodium: 125mg

SIDES

KALE & TOMATOES

 10 MINUTES  13 MINUTES  3 SERVINGS

INGREDIENTS

- 1 pound fresh kale, tough ends removed and chopped
- 2 teaspoons fresh lemon juice
- Salt and ground black pepper, as required
- 1 shallot, chopped
- 4 tomatoes, chopped
- 2 garlic cloves, minced
- 2 tablespoons olive oil

HOW TO MAKE IT

1. In a large frying pan, heat the oil over medium-high heat and sauté the shallot for approx. 4-5 minutes.
2. Next, add the garlic and sauté for approximately 1 minute.
3. Then add the kale and cook for approximately 6-8 minutes. Put in the tomatoes, lemon juice, salt and pepper and boil for approx. 3 minutes.
4. Take off the cooker and then serve hot.
5. Preparation tip: Put the vegetable preparation in a large bowl and put aside to cool.
6. Distribute the mixture among 3 airtight containers and refrigerate, partially covered, for 2 days. Rewarm in the microwave before serving.

NUTRITION Calories: 192 Fats: 9.7g Carbs: 23.9g Fiber: 4.3g Sugar: 4.4g Proteins: 6.3g Sodium: 126mg

SIDES

GREEN BEANS & MUSHROOMS MIX

15 MINUTES • 20 MINUTES • 2 SERVINGS

INGREDIENTS

- 1 cup frozen green beans
- Salt and ground black pepper, as required
- 1 (8-ounce) package white mushrooms, sliced
- 2 tablespoons olive oil
- 2 tablespoons yellow onion, minced
- 1/2 teaspoon garlic, minced
- 1 egg (optional)

HOW TO MAKE IT

1. Heat the oil in a pan over medium heat and fry the onion and garlic for approximately 1 minute. Meanwhile take a pot and boil one egg.

2. Then add the mushrooms and sauté for approximately 6-7 minutes. Mix in the green beans and cook for around 5-10 minutes or until desired doneness. Cut your egg in quarters. Serve together.

3. Meal prep tip: transfer the vegetable mixture to a large bowl and put aside to cool down. Split the mixture into 2 airtight containers. Put a lid on and store in the fridge for 2 days. Rewarm in the microwave before serving.

NUTRITION Calories: 166 Fats: 14.4g Carbs: 8.8g Fiber: 3.2g Sugar: 3.1g Proteins: 4.7g Sodium: 88mg

SIDES
YELLOW SQUASH & BELL PEPPERS MIX

15 MINUTES   10 MINUTES   3 SERVINGS

INGREDIENTS

- 1 1/2 teaspoons garlic, minced
- 1/4 cup water
- Salt and ground black pepper, as required
- 1 tablespoon ilive oil
- 3 cups yellow squash, sliced
- 1/2 cup onion, sliced
- 1/2 cup red bell pepper, seeded and julienned
- 1/2 cup green bell pepper, seeded and julienned

HOW TO MAKE IT

1. In a large frying pan, heat the oil on medium-high heat and fry the onion, peppers and pumpkin for around 4-5 minutes.
2. Then add the garlic and sauté for approx. 1 minute.
3. Now add the remaining ingredients and give them a stir. Lower the heat to medium and cook, mixing occasionally, for around 3-4 minutes. Serve hot.
4. Meal prep tip: Place the vegetable mixture into a large bowl and set aside to cool. Distribute the mixture among 3 airtight containers. Keep covered and chill for 2 days. Rewarm in the microwave before serving.

NUTRITION   Calories: 82 Fats: 5g Carbs: 9g Fiber: 2.2g Sugar: 4.8g Proteins: 2.1g Sodium: 64mg

SIDES

APPLE FLAVOURED BROCCOLI & CELERY

 15 MINUTES  17 MINUTES   3 SERVINGS

INGREDIENTS

- 1/2 cup red onion, chopped
- 1/4 cup celery stalk, chopped
- 1/4 cup homemade vegetable broth
- 2 apples, cored and sliced
- 1 tablespoon olive oil
- 2 garlic cloves, minced
- 2 cups small broccoli florets

HOW TO MAKE IT

1. In a large frying pan, warm the oil on a medium-high heat and fry the garlic for around 1 minute.
2. Then add the broccoli and continue to stir-fry for approx. 4-5 minutes.
3. Next, add the celery and onion and stir fry for around 4-5 minutes.
4. Add in the stock and cook for around 2-3 minutes.
5. Add the apple wedges and stir-fry for approx. 2-3 minutes. Serve hot.

NUTRITION Calories: 153 Fats: 5.3g Carbs: 27.4g Fiber: 5.8g Sugar: 17.5g Proteins: 2.9g Sodium: 93mg

CLASSIC ITALIAN PIZZA

 10 MINUTES    10 MINUTES    3 SERVINGS

INGREDIENTS

- 3 tablespoons Pizza sauce
- 1/2 cup, grated Mozzarella cheese
- 1/2 cup, halved Cherry tomatoes
- 1/8 teaspoon Italian blend seasoning
- 1/8 teaspoon Red pepper flakes
- 1 pizza crust, gluten-free

HOW TO MAKE IT

1. Heat the oven to 175 °C.
2. Divide the pizza sauce, cheese and cherry tomatoes among the flatbread.
3. Top with red pepper flakes and Italian seasoning.
4. Place in the preheated oven and bake for 10 minutes. Serve.

NUTRITION
Calories 195, Carbs 23g, Fat 7g, Protein 9g

HUMMUS & ZUCCHINI SUMMER PIZZA

 5 MINUTES    25 MINUTES    2 SERVINGS

INGREDIENTS

- 2 Tablespoon Chopped olives
- 1 cup Halved cherry tomatoes
- Sliced red onion
- Olive oil
- Sliced zucchini
- 4 Tablespoon Cheesy sprinkle
- 5 cups Classic hummus
- Gluten-free Pizza crusts

HOW TO MAKE IT

1. Switch the oven on to 400 degrees. Transfer the vegetables to a bowl and add salt and oil, swirling them around.
2. Put the two crusts together on a baking tray and put half of the hummus on each.
3. Cover with the vegetable mixture and some of the cheese and place in the oven.
4. Take out after 20 minutes and afterwards serve.

NUTRITION
Calories: 500 Carbs: 58g Fat: 25g Protein: 19g

Pizza

PAPRIKA SQUASH PIZZA WITH VEGETABLES

 25 MINUTES    21 MINUTES    4 SERVINGS

INGREDIENTS

- 1 tsp. cumin
- 1 tsp. oregano
- 1 tsp. paprika
- 3 cups butternut squash, fresh or frozen, cubed
- 1 tsp. red pepper flakes
- 2 tbsp. minced garlic
- 1 tbsp. olive oil
- Crust:
- 1 tsp. onion powder
- 2 cups dry French green lentils
- 1 tbsp. Italian seasoning
- 2 tbsp. minced garlic
- 2 cups water
- Toppings:
- 1 small purple onion, diced
- 1 tbsp. olive oil
- 1 cup chopped broccoli
- 1 medium green bell pepper, pitted, diced

HOW TO MAKE IT

1. Heat the oven to 350°F.
2. Make the French green lentils as per the method.
3. Put all the sauce ingredients in a food processor or mixer and puree on low speed until everything has blended and the resulting sauce looks creamy. Put the sauce aside into a small bowl.
4. Purge the food processor or blender; next, add all the ingredients for the crust and pulsate on high until a dough-like batter has formed.
5. Preheat a large deep skillet on medium-low heat and lightly grease with 1 tablespoon olive oil.
6. Push the crust dough into the pan to resemble a round pizza crust and cook until the crust is golden brown - around 5-6 minutes on each side.
7. Transfer the crust to a baking sheet covered with parchment paper.
8. Using a spoon, spread the top of the crust with the sauce and distribute the coating evenly over the pizza.
9. Place the pizza in the oven
10. Slice into 4 equal pieces and serve, or keep.

 Calories 258, Total Fat 9.2g, Saturated Fat 1.2g, Cholesterol 2mg, Sodium 21mg, Total Carbohydrate 38.3g, Dietary Fiber 9.7g, Total Sugars 6.2g, Protein 9g,

PIZZA

CHEESY SPINACH & RED PEPPERS PIZZA

---

10 MINUTES | 2 MINUTES | 6 SERVINGS

INGREDIENTS

- 1 small red onion, peeled and chopped
- 1/4 teaspoon of salt
- 1/2 teaspoon of red pepper flakes
- 5-ounce of spinach leaves, chopped
- 1 medium-sized red bell pepper, cored and sliced
- 1 1/2 teaspoons of minced garlic
- 1 cup of shredded vegan mozzarella
- 14-ounce of pizza sauce
- 12 inch of frozen gluten-free pizza crust, thawed
- 1/4 cup of chopped basil, fresh
- 1/2 teaspoon of dried thyme

HOW TO MAKE IT

1. Place a medium-sized non-stick pan over medium heat, pour in the oil and allow it to get hot.

2. Next, include the onion and garlic and let them cook for 5 minutes or until they soften.

3. Next, add the red pepper and simmer for 4 minutes or until it becomes tender-crisp.

4. Next, add the spinach, salt, red pepper, thyme and basil and give it a good stir.

5. Allow to cool for 3 to 5 minutes or until the spinach is wilted, then put aside until needed.

6. Grease a 4-quart slow cooker with non-stick cooking spray and put the pizza dough in.

7. Push the dough into the bottom and flatten it 1 inch up the sides.

8. Brush it with the pizza sauce, top with the spinach mixture and then evenly top with the cheese.

9. Scatter it with the red pepper flakes and the basil leaves and then cover it with the lid.

10. Connect the slow cooker and cook the pizza on a low heat setting for 1 1/2 to 2 hours, or till the crust is golden brown and the cheese is completely melted.

11. Once the pizza is ready, then transfer it to a chopping board, leave it to rest for 10 minutes and then cut it into slices to serve.

NUTRITION Calories: 250 Cal, Carbohydrates: 25g, Protein: 5g, Fats: 8g, Fiber: 1g.

PIZZA
ARTICHOKE PIZZA WITH CASHEWS SPREAD

 20 MINUTES    1 HOUR 50 MINUTES   6 SERVINGS

INGREDIENTS

- 2 tablespoons of sliced black olives
- 1 teaspoon of salt, divided
- 2 teaspoons of lemon juice
- 1 small green bell pepper, cored and sliced
- 2-ounce cashews
- 12 inch of frozen gluten-free pizza crust, thawed
- 3 tablespoon of olive oil, divided
- 4 fluid ounce of water
- 1/2 teaspoon of garlic powder
- 2 medium-sized tomatoes, sliced
- 1/2 teaspoon of dried oregano
- 2 tablespoons of nutritional yeast
- 1 mushroom, sliced
- 8-ounce of tomato paste
- 1/2 cup of sliced char-grilled artichokes

HOW TO MAKE IT

1. Place the cashews in a food processor; include the garlic powder, 1/2 teaspoon salt, the yeast, 2 tablespoons oil, lemon juice and water.
2. Blend until smooth and creamy, but adding a little water if needed.
3. Lubricate a 4 to 6 litre slow cooker with non-stick cooking spray and put the pizza dough in.
4. Press the dough into the base and distribute the tomato paste on top.
5. Dust it with garlic powder and oregano and top with the prepared cashew mixture.
6. Coat it with the mushrooms, peppers, tomatoes, artichoke slices, olives and then the rest of the olive oil.
7. Dust it with the oregano and the rest of the salt and put the lid on.
8. Connect the slow cooker and let it cook on a low heat setting for 1 to 1 1/2 hours, or untill the crust will be golden brown.
9. Once done, transfer the pizza to the chopping board, leave to rest for 10 minutes and cut into slices to serve.

NUTRITION Calories: 212 Cal, Carbohydrates: 39g, Protein: 16g, Fats: 5g, Fiber: 5g.

PIZZA

BLACK BEAN & AVOCADO SPICY PIZZA

 10 MINUTES    20 MINUTES    2 SERVINGS

INGREDIENTS

- 1 red onion
- 1 avocado
- 1 carrot, grated
- 2 prebaked gluten-free pizza crusts
- 1/2 cup Spicy Black Bean Dip
- 1 tomato, thinly sliced

NUTRITION

379 Calories 15g Fiber 13g Protein

HOW TO MAKE IT

1. Heat the oven to 400°F. Spread out the two crusts onto a large baking tray. Distribute half of the Spicy Black Bean Dip on top of each pizza crust.

2. Next, pile on the tomato slices with a pinch of pepper, to taste. Dust the grated carrot with the sea salt and gently massage with your hands.

3. Distribute the carrot on top of the tomato, then put in the onion.

4. Place the pizzas in the oven for 10 to 20 minutes, or until they are done to your liking. Garnish the cooked pizzas with avocado slices and a further pinch of pepper.

PIZZA BASE

 10 MINUTES    20 MINUTES    2 SERVINGS

INGREDIENTS

- 2 cups (250 g) gluten free flour
- 1/2 tbsp xanthan gum
- pinch of salt
- 1 tsp baking powder
- 3/4 cup (175 g) lukewarm water
- 1/3 oz (9 g) active dry yeast

HOW TO MAKE IT

1. In a big mixing bowl, combine all the dry components.

2. Grab a smaller bowl, stir all wet ingredients together.

3. Then mix the wet ingredients to the dry mixture and blend until the dough is very sticky.

4. Place the dough on top of a work surface (don't flour the surface!) and start working it. Continue for about 2 minutes.

5. Even if sticky, do not add flour to the dough.

- 1 tsp sugar
- 1 tbsp olive oil plus more for oiling the proofing bowl

NUTRITION

135 Cal, Carbohydrates: 15g, Protein: 6g, Fats: 5g, Fiber: 1g.

6. Transfer the dough to a well-greased large bowl, and cover with plastic wrap. Let rest for 2 - 3 hours.
7. Preheat the oven to 430°F and spread a light layer of polenta on a baking sheet.
8. Place the risen dough on the baking sheet and give it a shape of your likings. The middle of the pizza base should be 3mm thick, with a thicker outside edge.
9. Complete with your toppings and bake in a 430°F oven for 18-20 minutes.

BBQ TURKEY PIZZA

 20 MINUTES   2 MINUTES    6 SERVINGS

INGREDIENTS

- 1 1/2 teaspoons of salt
- 1 cup of barbecue sauce
- 2 cups of vegan mozzarella
- 12 inch of frozen gluten free pizza crust, thawed
- 3/4 teaspoon of ground black pepper
- 8 turkey thin slices (vegan: 1 cup tofu pieces)
- 1 tablespoon of olive oil
- 1 small red onion, peeled and sliced
- 1/4 cup of chopped cilantro

HOW TO MAKE IT

1. Place a large non-stick pan over medium heat, add 1 tablespoon of oil and allow it to get hot.
2. Vegan: Add the tofu pieces in a single layer, dust with 1 teaspoon of salt and black pepper and cook for 5 to 7 minutes or until crisp and golden brown on all sides. Put the tofu pieces in a bowl, add 1/2 cup of the barbecue sauce and swirl well to coat.
3. Lightly grease a 4- to 6-quart slow cooker with non-stick cooking spray and put the pizza dough in.
4. Push the dough into the bottom and pour in the remaining 1/2 cup of the barbecue sauce.
5. Evenly garnish it with tofu pieces or turkey slices and onion slices.
6. Top it with the mozzarella cheese and put the lid on.
7. Connect the slow cooker and let the pizza cook on medium-low heat for 1 to 1 1/2 hours, or till the crust is golden brown.
8. Transfer the pizza to a chopping board when it is ready, leave it to rest for 10 minutes and slice it to serve.

NUTRITION

135 Cal, Carbohydrates: 15g, Protein: 6g, Fats: 5g, Fiber: 1g.

107

DINNER

ALL SPICES EGGPLANT STEW

 35 MINUTES    42 MINUTES    4 SERVINGS

INGREDIENTS

- 1/2 cup golden raisins
- 1 tsp. cumin
- 1/4 tsp. chili powder
- 1/4 tsp Salt
- 1 tsp. olive oil
- 1 large eggplant
- 2 tbsp. turmeric
- 3/4 cup tomato sauce
- 1 cup dry chickpeas
- 1 cup vegetable broth
- 1 garlic clove, minced
- 1 cup dry green lentils
- 1/4 tsp pepper
- 1/2 tsp. allspice
- 1 large sweet onion, chopped
- 1 medium green bell pepper, seeded, diced

HOW TO MAKE IT

1. Heat the olive oil in a medium pan on a medium high heat.
2. Add the onions and sauté until they start to caramelize and soften, in 5-8 minutes.
3. Slice the eggplant into 1/2-inch eggplant cubes and put it to the pan along with the pepper, cumin, allspice, garlic, and turmeric.
4. Mix well the ingredients to blend everything evenly and warm up for around 4 minutes; then include the vegetable broth and tomato sauce.
5. Cover the pan, lower the heat, and simmer the ingredients until the eggplant is tender to the touch, or for around 20 minutes. You should be able to prick the cubes easily with a fork
6. Uncover and stir in the cooked chickpeas and green lentils, as well as the raisins and chili powder. Let the ingredients simmer until all the flavors have mixed together, or for around 3 minutes.
7. Save the stew for later, or serve in a bowl, season with salt and pepper, and enjoy!

NUTRITION

Calories 506, Total Fat 6g, Saturated Fat 0.8g, Cholesterol 0mg, Sodium 604mg, Total Carbohydrate 91.7g, Dietary Fiber 30.9g, Total Sugars 25.8g, Protein 26.7g

DINNER

BBQ GRITS & GREENS

 60 MINUTES    35 MINUTES    4 SERVINGS

INGREDIENTS

- 1/4 cup white onion, diced
- 2 garlic cloves, minced
- 1 tsp. salt
- 1/2 cup BBQ sauce
- 2 tbsp. olive oil
- 3 cups vegetable broth
- 1 cup gluten-free grits
- 3 cups collard greens, chopped
- 1 14-oz. package tempeh

HOW TO MAKE IT

1. Heat the oven to 400°F.
2. Cut the tempeh into thin slices and mix it with the BBQ sauce in a flat baking dish. Leave it aside and let marinate for up to 3 hours.
3. In a frying pan, heat 1 tablespoon of olive oil on a medium heat and then include the garlic and sauté until it is fragrant.
4. Pour the collard greens and 1/2 teaspoon of salt and fry until the collards are wilted and dark. Take out the pan from the heat and leave aside.
5. Cover the mixture of tempeh and BBQ sauce with aluminum foil. Arrange the baking dish into the oven and cook the ingredients for 15 minutes. Keep on baking for a further 10 minutes, until the tempeh is browned and crispy.
6.
7. Meanwhile, heat the remaining tablespoon of olive oil in the previously used frying pan on a medium heat.
8. Cook the onions until brown and fragrant, approximately 10 minutes.
9. Add the vegetable broth, bring to a boil; then lower the heat.
10. Slowly stir the grits into the simmering broth. Include the rest of 1/2 teaspoon of salt before covering the pan with a lid.
11. Leave the ingredients to simmer for around 8 minutes, until the grits are tender and creamy.
12. Serve and enjoy!

NUTRITION Calories 374, Total Fat 19.1g, Saturated Fat 3.5g, Cholesterol 0mg, Sodium 1519mg, Total Carbohydrate 31.1g, Dietary Fiber 2g, Total Sugars 9g, Protein 23.7g

DINNER

VEGAN CHILI

 10 MINUTES    10 MINUTES    4 SERVINGS

INGREDIENTS

- Kosher salt and cayenne pepper, to taste
- 2 ripe tomatoes, pureed
- 3 cups vegetable broth
- 2 bell peppers, diced
- 1 tablespoon paprika
- 1 large carrot, trimmed and diced
- 1 teaspoon mixed peppercorns
- 1 pound red black beans, soaked overnight and drained
- 2 bay leaves
- 3 tablespoons olive oil
- 2 cloves garlic, minced
- 1 large red onion, diced
- 2 tablespoons tomato ketchup
- 1 poblano pepper, minced

HOW TO MAKE IT

1. Cover the soaked beans with some fresh water and bring to a boil. Leave it to boil for around 10 minutes. Continue to cook for 50 to 55 minutes or until tender.

2. Heat the olive oil on a medium heat in a heavy-bottomed pot. When it is hot, sauté the onion, peppers and carrot.

3. Cook the garlic for about 30 seconds or until aromatic.

4. Include the rest of the ingredients along with the cooked beans. Leave it to simmer, mixing periodically, for 25 to 30 minutes or until cooked through.

5. Arrange into individual bowls and serve hot!

NUTRITION   Calories: 455; Fat: 10.5g; Carbs: 68.6g; Protein: 24.7g

DINNER

SAUTÉED CHICKPEA STEW

 10 MINUTES  10 MINUTES 4 SERVINGS

INGREDIENTS

- 1 bell pepper, chopped
- 1 onion, finely chopped
- 1 fennel bulb, chopped
- 3 cloves garlic, minced
- 2 tablespoons olive oil
- 2 ripe tomatoes, pureed
- 2 tablespoons fresh basil, roughly chopped
- 2 tablespoons fresh parsley, roughly chopped
- 2 cups vegetable broth
- 2 tablespoons fresh coriander, roughly chopped
- 14 ounces canned chickpeas, drained
- 1 teaspoon paprika
- Kosher salt and ground black pepper, to taste
- 1/2 teaspoon cayenne pepper
- 1 avocado, peeled and sliced

HOW TO MAKE IT

1. In a heavy bottomed pot, warm the olive oil over medium flame. Once it is hot, sauté the onion, fennel bulb and bell pepper for about 4 minutes.

2. Sauté the garlic for about 1 minute or until fragrant.

3. Add fresh herbs tomatoes, broth, chickpeas, cayenne pepper, paprika, salt, black pepper. Let it cook over low flame and toss occasionally, for about 20 minutes or until cooked.

4. Taste and adjust seasonings. Garnish with the fresh avocado slices and serve. Enjoy!

NUTRITION
Calories: 369; Fat: 18.1g; Carbs: 43.5g; Protein: 13.2g

DINNER

VEGETABLES & LENTIL MEDLEY

 10 MINUTES  10 MINUTES 4 SERVINGS

INGREDIENTS

- 1 carrot, chopped
- 3 tablespoons olive oil
- 1 bell pepper, diced
- 1 large onion, chopped
- 1 habanero pepper, chopped
- Kosher salt and black pepper, to taste
- 1 teaspoon ground cumin
- 3 cloves garlic, minced
- 1 teaspoon smoked paprika
- 1 (28-ounce) can tomatoes, crushed
- 4 cups vegetable broth
- 2 tablespoons tomato ketchup
- 3/4 pound dry red lentils, soaked overnight and drained
- 1 avocado, sliced

HOW TO MAKE IT

1. In a heavy bottomed pot, warm the olive oil over medium flame. Once warm, sauté the carrot, the onion, and the peppers for about 5 minutes.

2. Sauté the garlic for about 1 minute.

3. Combine the spices, tomatoes, ketchup, broth, and canned lentils. Let cook over low flame, mixing occasionally, for about 20 minutes.

4. Serve once garnished with the avocado slices.

NUTRITION   Calories: 475; Fat: 17.3g; Carbs: 61.4g; Protein: 23.7g

DINNER

CLASSIC ASIAN CHANA MASALA

 10 MINUTES    10 MINUTES   4 SERVINGS

INGREDIENTS

- 1 Kashmiri chile pepper, chopped
- 1 cup tomatoes, pureed
- 1 large shallot, chopped
- 4 tablespoons olive oil
- 1 teaspoon fresh ginger, peeled and grated
- 2 cloves garlic, minced
- 1 teaspoon garam masala
- 1 teaspoon coriander seeds
- 1/2 teaspoon turmeric powder
- 1/2 cup vegetable broth
- Sea salt and ground black pepper, to taste
- 16 ounces canned chickpeas
- 1 tablespoon fresh lime juice

HOW TO MAKE IT

1. Take a blender or a food processor, place the tomatoes, Kashmiri chili, shallots, and ginger and blend the ingredients into a paste.
2. In a saucepan, warm the olive oil over medium flame. Once hot, cook the paste you just made and the garlic for about 2 minutes.
3. Add the rest of the spices, broth, and chickpeas.
4. Bring the heat to a simmer. Continue to simmer for another 8 minutes.
5. Remove from heat. Squeeze fresh lime juice over each serving.

NUTRITION Calories: 305; Fat: 17.1g; Carbs: 30.1g; Protein: 9.4g

CHEF'S FAVOURITE RATATOUILLE

 15 MINUTES    40 MINUTES    4 SERVINGS

INGREDIENTS

- 2 tablespoons low-sodium vegetable broth
- 1 medium red onion, peeled and thinly sliced
- 1 large eggplant, stemmed and cut into 1/2-inch dice
- 2 cups cooked fava beans
- 2 Roma tomatoes, chopped
- 1 red bell pepper, seeded and diced
- 1 medium zucchini, diced
- 1/4 cup finely chopped basil
- Salt, to taste (optional)
- 2 cloves garlic, peeled and finely chopped
- Ground black pepper, to taste

HOW TO MAKE IT

1. Place the onion in a saucepan and sauté for 7 minutes or until it caramelizes.
2. Add the vegetable stock, eggplant and red bell pepper to the pan and sauté for another 10 minutes.
3. Combine the fava beans, tomatoes, zucchini and garlic to the pan and sauté for another 5 minutes.
4. Bring the flame to medium-low. Place the lid on the saucepan and cook for 15 minutes (make sure that the vegetables are soft). Stir the vegetables about halfway through cooking.
5. Transfer them to a serving platter. Drizzle with some basil, salt to taste and black pepper before serving.

NUTRITION Calories: 114 Fat: 1.0g Carbs: 24.2g Protein: 7.4g Fiber: 10.3g

SHAKES & SMOOTHIES

115

SUMMER STRAWBERRY SHAKE

🧤 10 MINUTES   🥄 0 MINUTES   🍴 1 SERVINGS

INGREDIENTS

- 1 cup of strawberries
- 2 cups of water
- 1 tablespoon of flaxseed oil
- 2 scoops of vanilla Protein powder

HOW TO MAKE IT

1. Add all the ingredients in a blender as listed and blend until smooth.
2. Serve and Enjoy!

NUTRITION   Calories: 303 Protein: 35g Carbs: 15g Fat: 11g

CHOCOLATE COFFEE POWER SHAKE

🧤 10 MINUTES   🥄 0 MINUTES   🍴 1 SERVINGS

INGREDIENTS

- Vegan Protein powder
- 2 scoops of chocolate
- 1/2 cup of low-Fat milk
- 1 tablespoon of instant coffee
- 1 cup of water

HOW TO MAKE IT

1. Add all the ingredients in a blender as listed and blend until smooth.
2. Serve and Enjoy!

NUTRITION   Calories 299 Protein: 42g Carbs: 14g Fat: 6g

SHAKES

GREEK YOGURT EXOTIC SHAKE

 10 MINUTES    0 MINUTES    1 SERVINGS

INGREDIENTS

- 1 cup chopped fresh pineapple
- 1 banana
- 4 mixed berries
- 1 scoop of vanilla vegan Protein powder
- 1 tablespoon low-Fat Greek yogurt

HOW TO MAKE IT

1. Add all the ingredients in a blender as listed and blend until smooth.
2. Serve and Enjoy!

NUTRITION   Calories: 355 Protein: 23g Carbs: 65g Fat: 3g

COCO ALMOND FRESH SMOOTHIE

 10 MINUTES    0 MINUTES    1 SERVINGS

INGREDIENTS

- 1 1/2 cups water
- 17 chopped almonds
- 1/2 teaspoon coconut extract
- 1 scoop chocolate Protein powder

HOW TO MAKE IT

1. Add all the ingredients in a blender as listed and blend until smooth.
2. Serve and Enjoy!

NUTRITION   Calories: 241 Protein: 24g Carbs: 6g Fat: 13g

VANILLA BLUEBERRIES FRESH SHAKE

 10 MINUTES  0 MINUTES  1 SERVINGS

INGREDIENTS

- 2 scoops of vanilla Protein powder
- 1 cup of ice
- 4 fresh or frozen blueberries
- 1 banana

HOW TO MAKE IT

1. Add all the ingredients in a blender as listed and blend until smooth.
2. Serve and Enjoy!

NUTRITION
Calories per serving: 329 Protein: 36g Carbs: 42g Fat: 2g

PROTEIN SHAKE FOR ATHLETES

 10 MINUTES  0 MINUTES  1 SERVINGS

INGREDIENTS

- 1 banana
- 3/4 cup of low-Fat milk
- 2 scoops of vanilla vegan Protein powder
- 1/4 pound of rolled oats

HOW TO MAKE IT

1. Add all the ingredients in a blender as listed and blend until smooth.
2. Serve and Enjoy!

NUTRITION
Calories per serving: 566 Protein: 59g Carbs: 69g Fat: 6g

SWEET PINK SMOOTHIE

 10 MINUTES    0 MINUTES    1 SERVINGS

INGREDIENTS

- 1/2 cup frozen raspberries
- 1 frozen banana
- 1/2 cup peeled and diced beets
- 1 tablespoon maple syrup
- 1 cup unsweetened almond milk

HOW TO MAKE IT

1. Combine all the ingredients in a blender as listed and blend until smooth.
2. Serve and Enjoy!

NUTRITION   Calories: 130, Protein 9 g, Fat 3 g, Carbs 28 g, Fiber 11 g

FRESH GREEN AND LEAN SHAKE

 10 MINUTES    0 MINUTES    1 SERVINGS

INGREDIENTS

- 1/2 banana, sliced
- 2 cups spinach or other greens, such as kale
- 1 cup sliced berries of your choosing, fresh or frozen
- 1 orange, peeled and cut into segments
- 1 cup unsweetened soy milk
- 1 cup ice

HOW TO MAKE IT

1. Get a blender, mix all the ingredients together.
2. Activate the blender on low speed, and gradually increase the speed until the it results smooth.

NUTRITION   Calories: 100, Protein 4 g, Fat 3 g, Carbs 20 g, Fiber 10 g

KALE HEALTHY SMOOTHIE

🧤 10 MINUTES 🥄 0 MINUTES 🍴 1 SERVINGS

INGREDIENTS

- 3/4 cup frozen blueberries
- 1 cup roughly chopped kale
- 1 tablespoon maple syrup
- 1 cup unsweetened soy milk
- Juice of 1 lemon

HOW TO MAKE IT

1. Add all the ingredients in a blender as listed and blend until smooth.
2. Serve and Enjoy!

NUTRITION Calories: 303 Protein: 35g Carbs: 15g Fat: 11g Calories: 95, Protein 5 g, Fat 6 g, Carbs 22 g, Fiber 11 g

CINNAMON SHAKE

🧤 10 MINUTES 🥄 0 MINUTES 🍴 1 SERVINGS

INGREDIENTS

- 1 tablespoon ginger, fresh & grated Pinch cardamom
- 1/4 teaspoon cinnamon
- 1 tablespoon chia seeds
- 1 cup alfalfa sprouts
- 2 medjool dates, Pitted
- 1 cup water
- 1 banana
- 1/2 cup coconut milk, unsweetened

HOW TO MAKE IT

1. Add all the ingredients in a blender as listed and blend until smooth.
2. Serve and Enjoy!

NUTRITION Calories: 210, Protein 8 g, Fat 9 g, Carbs 25g, Fiber 10 g

VEGAN TOFU SMOOTHIE

 10 MINUTES  0 MINUTES  1 SERVINGS

INGREDIENTS

- 1 banana
- 1 cup fresh or frozen berries
- 1 scoop vegan Protein powder
- 3/4 cup water or nondairy milk
- 1/4 cup rolled oats, or 1/2 cup cooked quinoa
- 3 ounces tofu
- 1 tablespoon flaxseed/chia seeds
- 1 handful fresh spinach or lettuce
- 1 chunk cucumber
- Coconut water to replace some of the liquid

HOW TO MAKE IT

1. Get a blender, combine berries, a banana, water, and your choice of vegan protein.
2. Blend for around 50 seconds until creamy and smooth. Fell free to add more water according to your texture preferences.

Nutrition Kcal: 180, Protein 18 g, Fat 5 g, Carbs 30 g, Fiber 11 g

SUNNY EXOTIC SMOOTHIE

 10 MINUTES  0 MINUTES 1 SERVINGS

INGREDIENTS

- 1 carrot, peeled & chopped 1 cup strawberries
- 1 cup peaches, chopped
- 1 banana, frozen & sliced
- 1 cup mango, chopped
- 1 cup water

HOW TO MAKE IT

1. Add all the ingredients in a blender as listed and blend until smooth.
2. Serve and Enjoy!

Nutrition Calories: 240, Protein 5 g, Fat 3 g, Carbs 70 g, Fiber 13 g

GREEN ENERGY SHAKE

 10 MINUTES  0 MINUTES  1 SERVINGS

INGREDIENTS

- 1 bunch kale, spinach, Swiss chard
- 1 bunch cilantro
- 1 tablespoon agave nectar
- 2 cucumbers, chopped and peeled
- 1 lemon, outer yellow peeled
- 1 orange, peeled
- 1 lime, peeled
- 1/2 cup ice

HOW TO MAKE IT

1. Add all the ingredients in a blender as listed and blend until smooth.
2. Serve and Enjoy!

NUTRITION Calories: 3180 Fat: 15g Carbohydrates: 8g Protein: 5g

ANTI-AGING TREASURE

 10 MINUTES  0 MINUTES 1 SERVINGS

INGREDIENTS

- 2 brazil nuts
- 2 cups wild blueberries, frozen
- 1 orange, peeled and cut in half
- 1 tablespoon flaxseeds
- 2 cups kale, roughly chopped
- 1 1/2 cups cold coconut water

HOW TO MAKE IT

1. Get a blender, combine fruit, kale, nuts and flaxseeds.
2. Add coconut water.
3. Blend for around 50 seconds until creamy and smooth.
4. Fell free to add more coconut water according to your texture preferences.

NUTRITION Calories 299 Protein: 42g Carbs: 14g Fat: 6g

SHAKES

COCO TURMERIC JUICE

 10 MINUTES    0 MINUTES    1 SERVINGS

INGREDIENTS

- 1 tablespoon coconut oil
- 1/2 cup pineapple, diced
- 1 teaspoon ground turmeric
- 1 banana, frozen
- 2 teaspoons chia seeds
- 1 cup of coconut milk

HOW TO MAKE IT

1. Add all the ingredients in a blender as listed and blend until smooth.
2. Serve and Enjoy!

NUTRITION Calories: 430 Fat: 30g Carbohydrates: 10g Protein: 7g

ACAI RECHARGE SHAKE

 10 MINUTES    0 MINUTES    1 SERVINGS

INGREDIENTS

- Water as needed
- 1-2 scoops vanilla Whey Protein
- 1/2 cup unsweetened nut milk
- 1 tablespoon unrefined coconut oil
- 1 tablespoon chia seeds
- 1/4 cup frozen blueberries
- 1/2 stick frozen acai puree
- 1 tablespoon almond butter

HOW TO MAKE IT

1. Add all the ingredients in a blender as listed and blend until smooth.
2. Serve and Enjoy!

NUTRITION Calories: 162 Fat: 14g Carbohydrates: 10g Protein: 3g

SHAKES

SKIN GLOW SUPER SHAKE

 10 MINUTES  0 MINUTES  1 SERVINGS

INGREDIENTS

- 2 cups kale
- 1 cup mango, chopped
- 1/2 avocado, sliced
- 1 cup pineapple, chopped
- 2 frozen bananas sliced
- 1 tablespoon flax
- 1/2 cup of coconut water

HOW TO MAKE IT

1. Add all the ingredients in a blender as listed and blend until smooth.
2. Serve and Enjoy!

NUTRITION Calories: 430 Fat: 40g Carbohydrates: 20g Protein: 10g

BREAKFAST POWER SHAKE

 10 MINUTES  0 MINUTES  1 SERVINGS

INGREDIENTS

- 1 cup unsweetened soy milk
- 2 tablespoons lemon juice
- 1/2 medium banana, ripe
- 1 cup packed spinach
- 2 tablespoons smashed avocado
- 1 tablespoon sunflower seeds

HOW TO MAKE IT

1. Add all the listed ingredients to a blender.
2. Blend until you have a smooth and creamy texture.
3. Serve chilled and enjoy!

NUTRITION Calories: 401 Fat: 42g Carbohydrates: 4g Protein: 2g

SHAKES

125

LEMONY MINTY BERRIES

 10 MINUTES    0 MINUTES   1 SERVINGS

INGREDIENTS

- Handful of mint
- 1 teaspoon chia seeds
- 1 cup strawberries
- 1 cup blueberries
- 1 tablespoon lemon juice
- 1 cup of coconut water

HOW TO MAKE IT

1. Get a blender, combine berries, seeds, some mint for extra flavor. Blend.
2. Add coconut water and lemon juice.
3. Blend for around 50 seconds until creamy and smooth.
4. Fell free to add more coconut water according to your texture preferences.

NUTRITION   Calories: 169 Fat: 13g Carbohydrates: 11g Protein: 6g

HEALTHY VEGGIE JUICE

 10 MINUTES    0 MINUTES    1 SERVINGS

INGREDIENTS

- 1 cup of coconut water
- 1 carrot, chopped
- 1 cup kale
- Lemon juice, 1 lemon
- 1 green apple, core removed and chopped

HOW TO MAKE IT

1. Combine all the listed ingredients in a blender.
2. Blend until you have a smooth and creamy texture.
3. Serve cold and enjoy!

NUTRITION   Calories: 116 Fat: 5g Carbohydrates: 14g Protein: 6g

DESSERTS & DELIGHTS

COCO-CINNAMON BALLS

 5 MINUTES    15 MINUTES   12 SERVINGS

INGREDIENTS

- 1 cup coconut shreds
- 1 cup coconut butter softened
- 1 cup coconut milk canned
- 1 tsp pure vanilla extract
- 1/2 tsp nutmeg
- 3/4 tsp cinnamon
- 2 Tbsp coconut palm sugar

HOW TO MAKE IT

1. Combine all ingredients (minus the coconut shreds) in a heated bath - bain-marie.
2. Cook and stir until all ingredients are soft and well blended.
3. Take the bowl from heat, place into another bowl, and refrigerate until the mixture is firm.
4. Shape the cold coconut mixture into balls, and roll each one in the shredded coconut.
5. Seal them into a container, and store in a refrigerator up to one week.

NUTRITION Calories: 247 Total Fat: 7g Saturated Fat: 2g Cholesterol: 17mg Sodium: 563mg Carbohydrates: 33g Fiber: 3g

Desserts

WALNUT APPLE BAKE

 20 MINUTES  25 MINUTES  6 SERVINGS

INGREDIENTS

For the filling

- 4 to 5 apples, cored and chopped
- 2 to 3 tablespoons unrefined sugar (coconut, date, sucanat, maple syrup)
- 1/2 cup unsweetened applesauce, or 1/4 cup water
- Pinch sea salt
- 1 teaspoon ground cinnamon

For the crumble

- 2 tablespoons maple syrup
- 2 tablespoons almond butter, or cashew or sunflower seed butter
- 1 1/2 cups rolled oats
- 1/2 teaspoon ground cinnamon
- 1/2 cup walnuts, finely chopped
- 2 to 3 tablespoons unrefined granular sugar (coconut, date, sucanat)

HOW TO MAKE IT

1. Preparing all the ingredients listed.
2. Preheat your oven to 350°F.
3. Place the apples and applesauce on a baking tray, sprinkle with sugar, cinnamon, and salt. Mix well to combine.
4. Take a bowl, blend together the nutty butter you prefer and maple syrup until the mixture results smooth and soft. Add the oats, walnuts, cinnamon, and sugar and mix well using your hands. I suggest you to mix the oats and the walnuts in a small food processor to obtain crumbles.
5. Sprinkle the nutty mixture over the apples, and place the tray in the oven.
6. Bake for about 20 to 25 minutes, the fruit has to be soft and the toppings brownish.

NUTRITION Calories 195, Fat 7 g, Carbohydrates 6 g, Sugar 2 g, Protein 24 g, Cholesterol 65 mg

CASHEW-CHOCOLATE TRUFFLES

5 MINUTES   15 MINUTES   12 SERVINGS

INGREDIENTS

- 1 cup raw cashew, soaked in water overnight
- 1 cup unsweetened shredded coconut, divided
- 2 tablespoons coconut oil
- 1 to 2 tablespoons cocoa powder, to taste
- 3/4 cup pitted dates

HOW TO MAKE IT

1. Combine the cashews in a food processor with dates, 1/2 cup of shredded coconut, cocoa powder and coconut oil. When they're fully amalgamated it will look like chunky cookie dough. Scatter the remaining 1/2 cup of shredded coconut on a plate.

2. Create tablespoon-size balls with the obtained mixture and roll them on the plate and cover with the shredded coconut.

3. Transfer to a paper towel or baking sheet. Repeat the process to make 12 truffles.

4. Place the truffles in the refrigerator for 1 hour to set. Transfer the truffles to a sealed freezer-safe bag or container.

NUTRITION   Calories 160   Fat 1 g   Carbohydrates 1 g   Sugar 0.5 g   Protein 22 g   Cholesterol 60 mg

BANANA CHOCOCUPCAKES

 20 MINUTES   20 MINUTES   1 SERVINGS

INGREDIENTS

- 3 medium bananas
- 2 tablespoons almond butter
- 1 cup non-dairy milk
- 1 teaspoon pure vanilla extract
- 1 teaspoon apple cider vinegar
- 1/2 cup rolled oats
- 1 1/4 cups oat flour
- 1 teaspoon baking powder
- 1/2 teaspoon baking soda
- 1/4 cup chia seeds, or sesame seeds
- 1/2 cup unsweetened cocoa powder
- 1/4 cup coconut sugar (optional)
- 1/4 cup dark chocolate chips, dried cranberries, or raisins (optional)
- Pinch sea salt

HOW TO MAKE IT

1. Preheat the oven to 350°F. Line two 6-cup muffin tins with paper muffin cups.

2. Put the bananas, almond butter, vinegar, milk, and vanilla in a blender and mix until smooth. Alternatively, stir together in a large bowl until soft and creamy.

3. In a large bowl, put the flour, sugar (if using), baking powder, oats, cocoa powder, chia seeds, baking soda, salt, and chocolate chips and stir to combine.

4. Mix the wet and dry ingredients together, stirring as little as possible. After spooned into muffin cups, bake for 20 to 25 minutes.

5. Take the cupcakes out of the oven. They'll be very moist, so let them cool completely before removing them from the muffin tins.

NUTRITION   Calories 295 Fat 17 g Carbohydrates 4 g Sugar 0.1 g Protein 29 g Cholesterol 260 mg

Desserts

FRUIT SALAD WITH MINT SCENT

 5 MINUTES    15 MINUTES    12 SERVINGS

INGREDIENTS

- 2 cups chopped pineapple
- 2 cups raspberries
- 2 cups chopped strawberries
- 1 cup blueberries
- 1/4 cup lemon juice (about 2 small lemons)
- 4 teaspoons maple syrup or agave syrup
- 8 fresh mint leaves

HOW TO MAKE IT

1. In a mason jar add the ingredients in this order: 1 tablespoon of lemon juice, 1 teaspoon of maple syrup, 1/2 cup of strawberries, 1/2 cup of raspberries, 1/2 cup of pineapple, 1/4 cup of blueberries, and 2 mint leaves.

2. Repeat for 3 more jars.

3. Close the jars tightly with lids and place them in the refrigerator for up to 3 days.

NUTRITION Calories 339 Fat 17.5 g Carbohydrates 2 g Sugar 2 g Protein 44 g Cholesterol 100 mg

MANGO COCONUT CREAM PIE

 20 MINUTES    25 MINUTES    6 SERVINGS

INGREDIENTS

- For the crust:
- 1 cup cashews
- 1 cup soft pitted dates
- 1/2 cup rolled oats
- For the filling:
- 1 cup canned coconut milk
- 2 large mangos, peeled and chopped, or about 2
- cups frozen chunks
- 1/2 cup unsweetened shredded coconut
- 1/2 cup water

HOW TO MAKE IT

1. Put all the ingredients for the crust in a food processor and pulse until it attaches together. Alternatively, chop the ingredients as finely as possible and use 1/2 cup cashew or almond butter instead of half the cashews, for softness.

2. Compress the mixture firmly into an 8-inch pie or springform pan.

3. Set all the filling ingredients in a blender and purée for about 1 minute or until creamy thick.

4. Pour the resulting filling into the crust, using a rubber spatula to level the top. Place the pie in the freezer until set, after about 30 minutes. Take it out about 15 minutes before serving, for it to soften up.

5. Once set, cover with Coconut Whipped Cream scooped on top of the pie. Complete it with a sprinkle of toasted shredded coconut.

NUTRITION   Calories 545 Fat 39.6 g Carbohydrates 9.5 g Sugar 3.1 g Protein 43 g Cholesterol 110 mg

Desserts

BERRIES VANILLA RICE PUDDING

5 MINUTES   15 MINUTES   12 SERVINGS

INGREDIENTS

- 1 cup short-grain brown rice
- 4 cups nondairy milk, plus more as needed
- 4 tablespoons unrefined sugar or pure maple syrup
- 2 cups water
- 1 teaspoon vanilla extract (use 1/2 teaspoon if you use vanilla milk)
- 1/2 cup frozen berries
- Pinch of salt

HOW TO MAKE IT

1. Combine the rice, milk, water, vanilla, and salt in your electric pressure cooker's cooking pot.
2. Close and lock the lid, and cook on High Pressure for 30 minutes.
3. Once cooking is concluded, let the pressure release naturally for about 20 minutes.
4. Remove the lid, mix in the berries and let it rest for the next 10 minutes with the lid on loosely. Serve, adding more milk as desired.

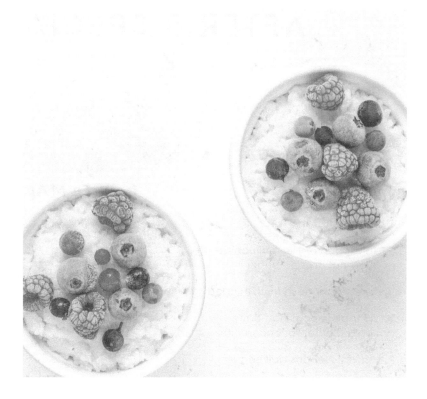

NUTRITION   Calories 420 Fat 27.4 g Carbohydrates 2 g Sugar 0.3 g Protein 46.3 g Cholesterol 98 mg

COCONUT CHIA PUDDING WITH LIME

 20 MINUTES    25 MINUTES    6 SERVINGS

INGREDIENTS

- Zest and juice of 1 lime
- 1 (14-ounce) can coconut milk
- 1 to 2 dates, or 1 tablespoon coconut
- 1 tablespoon maple syrup,
- 2 tablespoons chia seeds
- 2 teaspoons matcha green tea powder

HOW TO MAKE IT

1. Make a smooth mixture of all ingredients blending them in a blender.
2. Let it chill for about 20 minutes in the fridge.
3. Serve topped with one or more of the topping ideas: blueberries, blackberries, sliced strawberries, or toasted unsweetened coconut.

NUTRITION Calories 381 Fat 17.1 g Carbohydrates 4.1 g Sugar 0.6 g Protein 50.6 g Cholesterol 358 mg

AFTER 8 SPECIAL SORBET

 20 MINUTES    25 MINUTES    6 SERVINGS

INGREDIENTS

- 1 banana, frozen
- 1 tablespoon organic almond butter, or other nut or seed butter
- 2 tablespoons fresh mint, minced
- 2 to 3 tablespoons non-dairy chocolate chips, or cocoa nibs
- 2 to 3 tablespoons goji berries
- 1/4 cup or less non-dairy milk (only if needed)

HOW TO MAKE IT

1. Put the banana, almond butter, and mint in a blender and purée until smooth.
2. If you need to soften it up, add the non-dairy milk (but be aware this will make the texture less solid).
3. Pulse the goji berries and chocolate chips into the mix so they're roughly chopped up.

NUTRITION Calories 299 Fat 16 g Carbohydrates 3 g Sugar 6 g Protein 38 g Cholesterol 108 mg

PEACH-MANGO CRUMBLE

 5 MINUTES  15 MINUTES 12 SERVINGS

INGREDIENTS

- 1 cup gluten-free rolled oats
- 3 cups of chopped fresh or frozen mangos
- 3 cups of chopped fresh or frozen peaches
- 1/2 cup shredded coconut, sweetened or unsweetened
- 4 tablespoons unrefined sugar or pure maple syrup, divided
- 2 tablespoons coconut oil or vegan margarine

HOW TO MAKE IT

1. Toss together the mangos, peaches, and 2 tablespoons of sugar in a 6- to 7-inch round baking dish. In a blender, combine coconut, oats, coconut oil, and remaining 2 tablespoons of sugar, and pulse until thoroughly mixed. (In case you opt for maple syrup, start with just the syrup and add coconut oil only if the mixture isn't sticking together.)

2. Spatter the oat mixture over the fruit blend.

3. Cover the dish with aluminum foil.

4. Pour in your electric pressure cooker's cooking pot a cup or two of water. Lower the pan onto a trivet, lock the lid and set on high pressure for 6 minutes.

5. When the cooking is finished, quick release the pressure and remove the lid.

6. Let it chill for a few minutes before carefully lifting out the dish. Scoop out portions to serve.

NUTRITION   Calories 275 Fat 19 g Carbohydrates 19 g Sugar 4 g Protein 14 g Cholesterol 60 mg

136

ENERGY BITES 1 - CRANBERRY

 20 MINUTES    25 MINUTES    6 SERVINGS

INGREDIENTS

- 1 tablespoon chia seeds
- 2 tablespoons almond butter, or cashew or sunflower seed butter
- 1/4 cup sesame seeds, toasted
- 2 tablespoons maple syrup, or brown rice syrup 3/4 cup cooked quinoa
- 1 tablespoon dried cranberries
- 1/2 teaspoon almond extract, or vanilla extract Zest of 1 orange
- 1/4 cup ground almonds

HOW TO MAKE IT

1. Mix together the nut or seed butter and syrup in a medium bowl until smooth and soft. Mix in the rest of the ingredients, and stir to make sure the density is holding together in a ball.

2. Shape the mix into 12 balls.

3. Place them on a baking sheet lined with parchment or waxed paper and set in the fridge for about 15 minutes. If the mixture is not holding together, it's likely because of the moisture content of your cooked quinoa. Add more nut or seed butter blended with syrup until it all sticks together.

NUTRITION   Calories 493 Fat 33 g Carbohydrates 8 g Sugar 9 g Protein 47 g Cholesterol 135 mg

ENERGY BITES 2 - ALMONDS & DATES

 5 MINUTES  15 MINUTES  12 SERVINGS

INGREDIENTS

- 1/4 cup non-dairy chocolate chips
- 3/4 cup ground almonds
- 1 cup dates, pitted
- 1/4 cup chia seeds
- 1 cup unsweetened shredded coconut

HOW TO MAKE IT

1. Blend the ingredients in a blender until crumbly and sticking together. Alternatively, you can mash soft Medjool dates. If you're using harder baking dates, you'll have to soak them and then try to purée them in a blender. Use the softest dates you can find (Medjool dates are the best for this purpose).

2. Shape the mix into 24 balls and arrange them on a baking sheet lined with parchment or waxed paper. Put in the fridge to set for about 15 minutes.

NUTRITION Calories 171 Fat 4 g Carbohydrates 7 g Sugar 7 g Protein 22 g Cholesterol 65 mg

PUMPKIN PIE CUPS

 20 MINUTES    25 MINUTES    6 SERVINGS

INGREDIENTS

- 1 cup canned pumpkin purée
- 6 tablespoons unrefined sugar or pure maple syrup (less if using sweetened milk), plus more for sprinkling
- 1/2 teaspoon pumpkin pie spice
- 1/4 cup almond flour
- 1 cup nondairy milk
- Pinch salt

HOW TO MAKE IT

1. Stir together the milk, pumpkin, pumpkin pie spice, sugar or syrup, flour, and salt in a medium bowl.
2. Pour the mixture into 4 heat-proof ramekins.
3. Place a trivet in the bottom of your electric pressure cooker's pot and pour in a cup or two of water. Set the ramekins onto the trivet, piling them if needed (3 on the bottom, 1 on top).
4. Lock the lid, and cook on High Pressure for 6 minutes.
5. When cooking is finished, quickly release the pressure and remove the lid. Let chill for a few minutes before carefully lifting out the ramekins with oven mitts. Let it rest for at least 10 minutes before serving.

NUTRITION   Calories 152 Fat 4 g Carbohydrates 4 g Sugar 8 g Protein 18 g Cholesterol 51 mg

Desserts

BROWNIES WITH RASPBERRIES

 5 MINUTES    15 MINUTES    12 SERVINGS

INGREDIENTS

- 3 ounces dairy-free dark chocolate
- 1/3 cup almond flour
- 1/2 cup applesauce
- 2 tablespoons unrefined sugar
- 1 tablespoon coconut oil or vegan margarine
- 1/2 teaspoon baking powder
- 1/2 cup fresh raspberries
- Pinch salt

HOW TO MAKE IT

1. Place a trivet in your electric pressure pot and pour in a cup or two of water. Select Sauté or Simmer.

2. In a large heat-proof ceramic bowl, mix the chocolate with the coconut oil. Place the bowl over the top of your pressure cooker, as you would with a double boiler.

3. Stir occasionally until the chocolate is melted. Once liquid turn off the pressure cooker.

4. Spoon and mix the applesauce and sugar into the chocolate mixture.

5. Add and stir the flour, salt and baking powder, just until mixed.

6. Pour the mixture into 3 heat-proof ramekins. Place them in a heat-proof dish and cover with aluminum foil. Carefully lower the dish onto the trivet. (You can also cover each ramekin with foil and place them straight on the trivet, with no dish.)

7. Lock the lid, and select High Pressure for 5 minutes.

8. Once cooking is complete, release the pressure, and remove the lid.

9. Let cool for a few minutes before carefully removing the dish, or ramekins, with oven mitts. Let it chill for a few minutes more before serving.

10. You can now top them with fresh raspberries and an extra drizzle of melted chocolate.

Nutrition   Calories 256 Fat 29 g Carbohydrates 1 g Sugar 0.5 g Protein 11 g Cholesterol 84 mg

DESSERTS

COCONUT-BANANA PUDDING

 20 MINUTES    25 MINUTES    6 SERVINGS

INGREDIENTS

- 1 (13.5-ounce) can full-Fat coconut milk
- 3 bananas, divided
- 1 teaspoon vanilla extract
- 1/4 cup organic cane sugar
- 2 pinches sea salt
- 1 tablespoon cornstarch
- Ground cinnamon, for garnish

HOW TO MAKE IT

1. Combine 1 banana, coconut milk, vanilla, sugar, cornstarch, and salt in a blender. Blend until soft and creamy.

2. Pour to a sauce pot and bring to boil over medium-high heat. As it boils reduce immediately to a simmer and whisk for 3 minutes, or until the mixture sticks to the spoon.

3. Transfer the mixture to a container and leave to chill for 1 hour. Cover and refrigerate 5 hours or overnight.

4. Before serving, slice the remaining 2 bananas and build your "lasagna": pudding, banana slices, pudding, and so on until you have 8-12 layers. Sprinkle with ground cinnamon.

NUTRITION   Calories 170 Fat 4 g Carbohydrates 34 g Sugar 14g Protein 9 g Cholesterol 14 mg

Desserts

141

SPICED APPLE CHIA PUDDING

 5 MINUTES    15 MINUTES   12 SERVINGS

INGREDIENTS

- 1/2 cup unsweetened applesauce
- 1/4 cup nondairy milk or canned coconut milk
- 1 tablespoon chia seeds
- 1/2 teaspoons unrefined sugar

HOW TO MAKE IT

1. Stir together the applesauce, milk, chia seeds, sugar, and cinnamon or pumpkin pie spice in a small bowl.
2. Enjoy as-is, or if you prefer the chia seeds softer, let it sit for 30 minutes before serving.

Nutrition   Calories 145, Fat 4 g, Carbohydrates 19 g, Sugar 9 g Protein 2 g, Cholesterol 26 mg

CARAMELIZED BANANAS

 5 MINUTES    15 MINUTES    12 SERVINGS

INGREDIENTS

- 2 bananas, peeled, halved crosswise and then lengthwise
- 2 tablespoons vegan margarine or coconut oil
- 2 tablespoons spiced apple cider
- 2 tablespoons dark brown sugar, demerara sugar, or coconut sugar
- Chopped walnuts, for topping

HOW TO MAKE IT

1. Melt the margarine over medium heat in a nonstick skillet. When smooth, add the bananas and cook for 2 minutes. Flip the bananas, and cook for 2 more minutes. Spatter the sugar and cider around the
2. bananas, and cook for 2 to 3 minutes, until the sauce thickens and caramelizes.
3. Scoop the bananas into dishes, and drizzle any remaining liquid in the skillet. Sprinkle with walnuts.

Nutrition   Calories: 413 Fat: 13g Saturated Fat: 4g Cholesterol: 98mg Carbohydrates: 64g Fiber: 5g Protein: 37g

SWEET & SALTED FUDGE

 20 MINUTES    25 MINUTES    6 SERVINGS

INGREDIENTS

- 6 tablespoons fair-trade unsweetened cocoa powder
- 3/4 cup creamy almond butter
- 1/3 cup coconut oil, softened or melted
- 1/2 cup maple syrup
- 1 teaspoon coarse or flaked sea salt

HOW TO MAKE IT

1. Line a double layer of plastic wrap in a loaf pan. Lay one layer horizontally in the pan, and the second layer vertically, both with a generous amount of overhang.

2. Gently mix together in a medium bowl the almond butter, maple syrup, and coconut oil until well mixed and smooth. Gently stir cocoa powder into the mixture until well combined and creamy.

3. Pour the blend into the prepared pan and sprinkle with the sea salt.

4. Bring the abundant edges of the plastic wrap over the top of the fudge to cover it completely. Put the pan in the freezer for at least 1 hour or overnight, until the fudge is firm.

5. Remove the pan from the freezer and lift the fudge out of the pan using the plastic-wrap overhangs to pull it out. Transfer carefully to a cutting board and cut into 1or2-inch pieces. Serve and enjoy!

NUTRITION   Calories 297 Fat 20.3 g Carbohydrates 4 g Sugar 5 g Protein 21 g Cholesterol 80 mg

Desserts

COCO BALLS

 10 MINUTES  5 MINUTES  12 SERVINGS

INGREDIENTS

- 2 oz coconut, finely shredded, unsweetened
- 1/2 cup shredded coconut
- 1/3 cup coconut butter softened
- 1/3 cup coconut oil melted
- 4 Tbsp coconut palm sugar

HOW TO MAKE IT

1. Process all ingredients, but shredded coconut in a blender. Mix until soft and well combined.
2. Make small balls from the mixture and roll in shredded coconut.
3. Place on a sheet lined with parchment paper and refrigerate overnight.
4. You can place the coconut balls into sealed container and keep in the fridge up to 7 days.

Nutrition

Calories: 247 Total Fat: 7g Saturated Fat: 2g Cholesterol: 17mg Carbohydrates: 33g Protein: 12g

DESSERTS

CHOCO VANILLA CAKE

 20 MINUTES    25 MINUTES    6 SERVINGS

INGREDIENTS

- 1 1/2 cups of almond flour
- 1/3 cup almonds finely chopped
- 1/4 cup of cocoa powder unsweetened
- 1/2 tsp baking soda
- 2 Tbsp almond milk
- 1/2 cup Coconut oil melted
- 2 tsp pure vanilla extract
- 1/3 cup brown sugar (packed)
- Pinch of salt

HOW TO MAKE IT

1. Preheat oven to 350 F. Line 9" cake pan with parchment paper, and grease with few drops of coconut oil.
2. Stir the chopped almonds, almond flour, cocoa powder, baking soda and salt in a bowl.
3. In a separate bowl stir the remaining ingredients. Combine the almond milk mixture with the almond flour mixture and mix well. Place the mixture in a prepared cake pan.
4. Bake for 30 to 32 minutes.
5. Remove from the oven, allow it to cool completely before serving.

NUTRITION Calories: 460 Total Fat: 32g Saturated Fat: 23g Cholesterol: 223mg Sodium: 902mg Carbohydrates: 16g Fiber: 5g Protein: 29g

145

VANILLA BANANA CAKE

 5 MINUTES   15 MINUTES   12 SERVINGS

INGREDIENTS

- 4 ripe bananas, in chunks
- 1/3 cup of almonds finely chopped
- 3 tbsp honey or maple syrup
- 1 tsp cinnamon
- 1 tsp pure vanilla extract
- 3/4 cup of self-rising flour
- 1/2 cup almond milk
- 1 tsp baking powder
- 1 pinch of salt
- Almond slices for decoration

HOW TO MAKE IT

1. Preheat the oven to 400 F (air mode). Soft up a cake mold with coconut oil.
2. Mash bananas with the fork. Add honey, vanilla, almond and mix well.
3. In a second bowl, stir flour, cinnamon, baking powder, the broken almonds, and salt, mix with a spoon.
4. Add the banana mixture, and stir until all ingredients are well combined. Transfer the mixture to the cake mold and sprinkle with sliced almonds.
5. Bake for 40-45 minutes or until a toothpick inserted comes out clean.
6. Remove from the oven, and allow the cake to cool down completely.

NUTRITION   Calories: 301, Total Fat: 8g, Saturated Fat: 1g Cholesterol: 99mg, Sodium: 08mg, Carbohydrates: 21g, Fiber: 4g, Protein: 26g

HOMEMADE COCOBANANA ICE CREAM

 20 MINUTES  25 MINUTES  6 SERVINGS

INGREDIENTS

- 2 large frozen bananas (chunks) 3 Tbsp honey extracted
- 1 cup coconut cream
- 1/4 tsp cinnamon powder
- 1/2 cup Inverted sugar

NUTRITION

Calories: 87 Cal Fat: 7 gCarbs: 9 g Protein: 1.5 g Fiber: 3.2 g

HOW TO MAKE IT

1. In a bowl, whisk the coconut cream with the inverted sugar.
2. In another bowl, whip the banana with honey and cinnamon.
3. Combine the coconut whipped cream with the banana mixture and mix thoroughly.
4. Cover the bowl and let cool in the refrigerator overnight. Remember to stir the mixture 3 to 4 times to prevent crystallization.

HEALTHY BUTTER-CLOUDS COOKIES

 20 MINUTES  25 MINUTES  6 SERVINGS

INGREDIENTS

- 2 tbsp chia seeds soaked in 4 tablespoons water
- 1/2 cup hazelnut butter softened
- 1/2 cup coconut butter softened
- 1/2 cup of granulated sugar
- 1/2 tsp pure vanilla extract
- 1/2 cup of brown sugar

HOW TO MAKE IT

1. Preheat oven to 360 F. Combine together hazelnut butter, coconut butter, and both sugars in a mixing bowl.
2. Whip with a mixer until smooth and sugar is blended well.
3. Add vanilla extract and the soaked chia seeds and stir.
4. Also add baking soda, flour and salt; beat until all ingredients are combined well.

- 1/2 tsp baking soda
- 1 cup of all-purpose flour
- 1/4 tsp salt

5. Shape dough into cookies by hand. Arrange them onto a baking sheet, and bake for about 10 minutes.
6. Take out the cookies from the oven and allow to cool completely.

NUTRITION
Calories: 731 Total Fat: 26g Saturated Fat: 17g Cholesterol: 169mg Sodium: 1167mg Carbohydrates: 56g Fiber: 5g, Protein: 45g

SPICED APPLE CHIA PUDDING

 5 MINUTES    15 MINUTES    12 SERVINGS

INGREDIENTS

- 1/2 cup coconut butter softened
- 1/2 cup cashew butter softened
- 1/2 cup of granulated sugar
- 1/2 cup of brown sugar
- 2 Tbsp chia seeds soaked in 4 tablespoons water
- 1/2 tsp pure vanilla extract
- 1/2 tsp baking soda
- 1/4 tsp salt
- 1 cup of all-purpose flour

HOW TO MAKE IT

1. Preheat oven to 360 F.
2. Add coconut butter, cashew butter, and both sugars in a mixing bowl.
3. Beat with a mixer until soft and sugar combined well.
4. Add soaked chia seeds and vanilla extract; beat. Add baking soda, salt, and flour; beat until all ingredients are combined well.
5. With your hands, shape dough into cookies. Arrange your cookies onto a baking sheet, and bake for about 10 minutes.
6. Remove cookies from the oven and allow to cool completely. Sprinkle with icing sugar and enjoy your cookies.
7. Place cookies in an airtight container and keep refrigerated up to 10 days.

NUTRITION
Calories: 731 Total Fat: 26g Saturated Fat: 17g Cholesterol: 169mg Sodium: 1167mg Carbohydrates: 56g Fiber: 5g, Protein: 45g

CHOCOMINT HAZELNUT

 20 MINUTES    25 MINUTES   6 SERVINGS

INGREDIENTS

- 1/2 cup coconut oil, melted
- 4 Tbsp cocoa powder
- 1/4 cup almond butter
- 3/4 cup brown sugar - (packed)
- 1 tsp vanilla extract
- 1 tsp pure peppermint extract pinch of salt
- 1 cup shredded coconut
- 1 cup hazelnuts sliced

HOW TO MAKE IT

1. Chop the hazelnuts in a food processor; set aside.
2. Fill the bottom of a double boiler with water and place it on low heat.
3. Put the coconut oil, cacao powder, almond butter, brown sugar, vanilla, peppermint extract, and salt in the top of a double boiler over hot (not boiling) water and constantly stir for 10 minutes.
4. Add hazelnuts and shredded coconut to the melted mixture and stir together.
5. Pour the mixture in a dish lined with parchment and freeze for several hours.
6. Remove from the freezer and cut into bars. Store in airtight container or freezer bag in a freezer. Let the bars at room temperature for 10 to 15 minutes before eating.

NUTRITION   Calories: 186 Total Fat: 4g Saturated Fat: 0g Cholesterol: 33mg Sodium: 783mg Carbohydrates: 23g Fiber: 6g, Protein: 19g

CONCLUSION

The union of Paleo and Vegan gave us one of the most complete and healthiest diet around today.

Pegan Diet promotes optimal health by reducing inflammation and balancing blood sugar, trying to be the most sustainable and environmental friendly as possible.

It is a great way to eat in a well balanced and complete way, and it's much easier to follow than any other very restrictive diet regimen; yet it will contribute to your general well being.

I hope you have found the perfect recipes to let you enjoy your road to eating in the right way!

To your health,

Renee

INDEX
in alphabetical order

Açaí Bowl	17
Acai Recharge Shake	123
After 8 Special Sorbet	134
Air-Fried Vegan Buffalo Cauliflower Wings	26
All Spices Eggplant Stew	108
Almond Butter Baked Potatoes	27
APPETIZER	20
Apple Flavoured Broccoli & Celery	99
Aromatic Broccoli &	86
Aromatic Garlic Baked Mashroom	93
Artichoke Filled Aubergine	16
Artichoke Pizza with Cashews Spread	104
Asian Roasted Almonds	25
Avocado & Chickpeas	42
Avocado & cod fillet Toast	13
Baked Pasta Bolognese & Cashew Besciamella	78
Balsamic Beet Burger	48
Balsamic Oven Baked Brussels Sprouts	92
Banana ChocoCupcakes	130
BBQ Grits & Greens	109
BBQ Sauce Chikpeas Coleslaw Wrap	67
BBQ turkey Pizza	106
Berries-Vanilla Rice Pudding	133
Berries & almond Butter Oats	18
Berries & Pistachio Butter Oats	15
Black Bean & Avocado Spicy Pizza	105
Black Beans Burger	49
Bok Choy Cumin Rice	75
Breakfast Power Shake	124
Broccoli Avocado Cream	80
Brownies with Raspberries	139
BRUNCH	13
BURGERS	47
Caramelized Bananas	141
Cashew Spread	14
Cashew-Chocolate Truffles	129
Cheesy Spinach & Red Peppers Pizza	103
Chef's Favourite Ratatouille	114
Chickpea Bonanza Salad Bites	41
Chinese Vegetables Noodles	79
Choco Vanilla Cake	144
Chocolate Coffee Power Shake	116
Cilandrolamb Wrap with almond Sauce	64
Cinnamon Banana Waffles	13
Cinnamon Rolls and	14
Cinnamon Shake	120
Classic Asian Chana Masala	113
Classic Asian Noodles	74
Classic Italian Pizza	101
Classic Vegan Burritos	45
Coco Almond Fresh Smoothie	117
Coco Balls	143
coco Turmeric Juice	123
Coco-Cauliflower Burgers	50
Coco-Cinnamon Balls	127
Coconut Chia Pudding with Lime	134
Coconut-Banana Pudding	140
Creamy Carrots Salad with Chickpeas	91
Creamy Coconut Kale Soup	83
Crispy Avocado Slices	24
Cumin Sweet Potato Tots	23
Curry Coated Carrots	94
Curry Mango Tahini Wraps	68
DESSERTS	127
DINNER	108
Energy Bites 1 - Cranberry	136
Energy Bites 2 - Almonds & Dates	137
Exotic Tofu Lettuce Wrapped	69
Fresh Green and Lean Shake	119
Fruit Salad With Mint Scent	131
Garlic Beet Medley	84
Garlic Leek Soup	82
Garlic Lentils Casserole	29
Garlic Okra Casserole	16

Geek Yogurt Exotic Shake	117	Sautéed Chickpea Stew	111
Geen Energy Shake	122	SIDES	90
Ginger & Onion Soup	80	Simple Lentil & Tomato Paste Wrap	63
Granny Herbs Veggies Soup	88	Simple Sweet Potato Burgers	51
Greek Fantasy Bowl	40	Simple Vegetables Noodles	72
Green Beans & Mushrooms Mix	97	Skin Glow Super Shake	124
Green Chicken Sandwich	35	SOUPS	80
Grilled Corn with Veganaise Coating	90	Soy and Mustard Seitan Burgers	56
Healthy Butter-Clouds Cookies	146	Soy Flavoured Red Cabbage Wrap	66
Healthy Veggie Juice	125	Soy Sauce & Sesame Spinach	94
Homemade CocoBanana Ice Cream	146	Special Veggie Salad with veal	38
Hummus & Zucchini Summer Pizza	101	Spiced Apple Chia Pudding	141
Hummus and Olive Wrap	61	Spiced Apple Chia Pudding	147
Italian Basil & Tomato Soup	84	Spicy Cauliflower Tacos	30
Kale & Tomatoes	96	Spicy Curry Pumpkin Soup	82
Kale Crunchy Chips	24	Spicy Pineapple & Kale Medly	85
Kale Healthy Smoothie	120	Spicy Vegetables Noodles with Siriracha Sauce	73
Kidney Bean Tasty Dip	21	Spinach Flax Meal Burgers	57
Lentil & Carrot Burgers	53	Summer Cups	42
Lentils, Farro & Mustard Salad	39	Summer Strawberry Shake	116
Lime Quinoa & chicken Salad	37	Sunny Exotic Smoothie	121
LUNCH	29	Sweet & Salted Fudge	142
Mango Coconut Cream Pie	132	Sweet Energy Potato Sushi	44
Marinated Ratatouille Skewers	90	Sweet Pink Smoothie	119
Mediterranean Vegetable Mix Wrap	62	Sweet Potatoes & Legumes Soup	81
Minty Tandory beef Wraps	60	Tacos with Tahini	36
Mushroom salmon Spicy Burger	55	Tamari chicken with Mushrooms	31
Mushroom Soup	86	Tandoori Chickpeas	20
Pakora Cream	87	Taste of India Bowl	32
Panko Air-Fried Ravioli	22	Tasty Artichoke & White Bean Sandwich	34
Paprika & Almond Butter Potato Patties	52	Tempeh & Black Beans Patties	58
Paprika Black Bean & Quinoa Lettuce Wrap	70	Tumeric Beans Burger	54
Paprika Favoured Sweet Potatoes	95	Tumeric Cauliflower	87
Paprika Squash Pizza with Vegetables	102	Vanilla Banana Cake	145
Pasta with Pesto Sauce	77	Vanilla Blueberries fresh Shake	118
PASTA	72	Vegan Buffalo Wrap	65
Peach-Mango Crumble	135	Vegan Chili	110
pizza base	105	Vegan Poppy Seed Scones	15
PIZZA	101	Vegan Tofu Smoothie	121
Protein Shake for Athletes	118	Vegetables & Lentil Medley	112
Pumpkin & Mushroom Risotto	43	walnut apple bake	128
Pumpkin Burgers	47	WRAPS	60
Pumpkin Pie Cups	138	Yellow Squash & Bell Peppers Mix	98
Rich Pumpkin Sauce Pasta	76	Zucchini Gratin	17
Royal Chickpea Sandwich	33		

152

Made in United States
Cleveland, OH
18 September 2025